A LONG WALK SOUTH

AN IRISHMAN'S TREK ON THE GR5

SEAN ROTHERY is an architect and architectural historian. Now retired, he is still active as a lecturer in Ireland and abroad. The author of many books and numerous articles, he is a lifelong lover of walking and mountaineering.

Email: seanandnualarothery@eircom.net

*For Eoin, Colm and Finuala
and in memory of Nuala*

A LONG WALK SOUTH

AN IRISHMAN'S TREK ON THE GR5

SEAN ROTHERY

The Collins Press

PUBLISHED IN PAPERBACK IN 2014 BY
The Collins Press,
West Link Park,
Doughcloyne,
Wilton,
Cork

First published in hardback 2001

A CIP record for this book is available from the British Library.

Paperback ISBN: 978-18488-9197-5
PDF eBook ISBN: 978-18488-9838-7
EPUB eBook ISBN: 978-18488-9839-4
Kindle ISBN: 978-18488-9840-0

Typesetting by Patricia Hope
Typeset in Sabon
Printed in Poland by Drukarnia Skleniarz

Contents

Castle, Beaufort, Luxembourg

LIST OF MAPS

Acknowledgements

My first thanks must be to those friends who volunteered to meet me and walk some way with me at various stages of the long journey. Their companionship was for those, albeit brief, periods enjoyable and nurturing and without their support I might have lost heart. They are, in order of appearance on the trail, Petra Kreb from Amsterdam, Nanno Huismann from Heerlin, Sally Keogh from Dublin and Nuala Rothery from Dublin. As well as the pleasure of their company they were the bearers of fresh supplies such as maps, books and clothes but above all, the meeting points with them stood out as eagerly anticipated, if often distant, goals.

I met many people along the way, at least in the latter stages of the trail, but a handful of fellow walkers shared a few days with me. My thanks to Sandrijn Vink from Utrecht whose company through the early parts of Lorraine was a pleasure. The all too short encounter with the Dutch couple, John and Marie Haandel from Blaricum, in Luxembourg, raised my spirits at a time when I felt I was the only person mad enough to plod daily the long distance walk. I crossed paths in the Vosges and again in the Jura with the young Frenchmen, François and Cristophe, and enjoyed the sharing over bottles of wine. There were many Dutch on the trail and I joined Yvonne Netenboom and Connie Van Zanten from Gravenzande for several stages in the Jura and they were agreeable dinner companions after many solitary evenings.

There must be a special thanks to the Belgian couple Mady and Jaques Bouckaert who showed such hospitality to Petra and myself when we invaded their Kalmthout home, hot and thirsty on that day in May.

Finally I am deeply grateful for the patient advice and careful editing skills of Jonathan Williams.

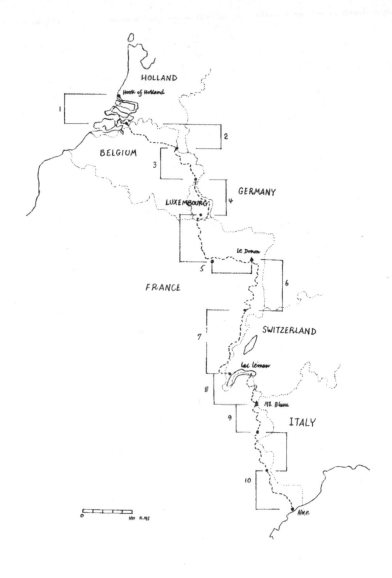

Map 1: Hook of Holland to Nice

11

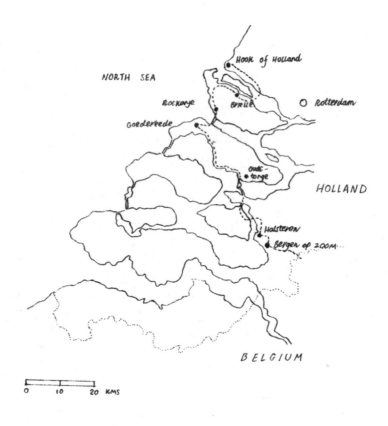

NORTH SEA

Hook of Holland

Rockanje

Brielle

Goedereede

O Rotterdam

Oude-tonge

HOLLAND

Halsteren

Bergen op Zoom

BELGIUM

0   10   20 KMS

Map 2: Holland

CHAPTER 1

The Lowlands – Dams and Dykes

10 May 1994

A grey sky and a colourless sea with waves breaking over a froth of yellow-white foam. I undressed on the deserted beach and ran naked into the cold ocean. Early morning on the coast of Holland and the start of my long walk from the North Sea to the Mediterranean. It was to be four months and a journey of nearly 2,300km before I could wade into the warm, blue bay at Nice. The sun came out as I crossed the dunes and stepped onto the pathway of the town park of the Hook of Holland. The first stage of the long-distance trail officially started at the railway station and ferry terminal, but it seemed more appropriate to begin at the water's edge and thus link the cold North to the warm South.

The idea of undertaking a long journey on foot had its genesis some three years before I was due to retire from a full-time academic career. My motives were mixed. A challenge, perhaps, to growing old? A celebration of freedom after over 40 years as a wage slave? The cliché 'because it was there' seemed reason enough since I am a long-time lover of mountains and wilderness. William Hazlitt's essay 'On going a journey', which I first read at fourteen, made a lasting impression.

The soul of a journey is liberty, perfect liberty, to think, feel, do just as one pleases.

The taking on of a reasonably hard physical task was given an added impetus by my attendance at a 'retirement course', organised with philanthropic zeal by the institution which had decreed that every worker over 65 was no longer capable or useful. The various speakers were harmless if anodyne, but the doctor, an overweight forty-something, who came on to lecture the 'senior citizens' about their health, was patronising with his admonition for us to take long walks, 'at least two or three miles'! I resolved there and then to go on a real journey, not quite a Patrick Leigh Fermor walk to Constantinople, but something nearly comparable and dramatic – a long journey on foot through space and time.

Leigh Fermor walked to the Danube and then on to Constantinople from the Hook of Holland in the 1930s. This was long before the vast road networks and monstrous traffic levels of the late twentieth century made such a journey today seem like madness. After the Second World War, the French were amongst the first to establish long-distance footpath routes through whole regions of their country. These were given the name *Grande Randonée* and cleverly linked up old bridle paths, forest trails, canal towpaths, riverbanks, transhumance paths, Roman roads, minor roads and mountain passes, to create a huge and intricate network of walking routes. One of the earliest of these was the *Grande Randonée Cinq*, popularly known as the GR5, which originally stretched from the northerly tip of the Vosges mountains, through the Jura, before traversing the French Alps to Nice. In the last two decades the GR5 was extended through Lorraine to the border of

Luxembourg and then northwards through the Ardennes and across Flanders to Holland. In the 1980s the Dutch extended the route to the Hook of Holland; thus making it the North Sea to the Mediterranean Long Distance Walking Trail – the E3.

In the 1960s, when the GR5 existed only as a waymarked route down the eastern side of France from Alsace in the north and southwards through the Alps, John Hillaby, the prince of long-distance walkers, saw the possibility of linking the seas of the North and the South. His book *Journey through Europe* was the story of that epic walk. Reading that account was an inspiration to me. The GR5 today, however, is substantially different, and longer, from the way Hillaby went and, except in a few places, notably the southern Ardennes and Luxembourg, the routes rarely match.

The clouds had now vanished. The sun was warm. Birdsong and the wild flowers of late spring made it a great start. A Dutch friend, Petra Kreb, had joined me for the first day of the journey and we set out strongly eastwards on smooth, hard and very flat paths.

A decision had to be made when planning the journey whether to seek companions for the whole trip or to attempt the walk alone. A solitary expedition was tempting, despite the obvious drawbacks – potential spells of loneliness, possible dangers and the real difficulties of carrying a heavy load and resupply of necessities. Hazlitt had no doubts about the merits of travelling alone:

One of the pleasantest things in the world is going a journey; but I like to go by myself. I can enjoy society in a room; but out of doors, nature is company enough for me. I am then never less alone than when alone.

Regarding dangers: I never felt unsafe, except when out in thunderstorms in the Alps, and companions would not have helped there. 'Were you not afraid of being alone?' was the question most asked before and after the trip. The equipment to be carried and the resupply of essential items were more serious problems. A compromise on the solitary journey was accepted where I would meet friends at different stages for companionship, as well as to provide me with maps, guidebooks or any replacement clothes. Petra was to rejoin me for two days in Belgium. An early stage rest-stop was Maastricht, where I would stay with another Dutch friend, Nanno Huismann, who lived in nearby Heerlen. He also had agreed to meet me for a day or so in the Ardennes. In Lorraine I was to meet an Irish friend, Sally Keogh, who would walk with me towards the foot of the Vosges mountains. Finally my wife, Nuala, along with Nanno, would join me for the first stage in the French Alps. I spent 110 days on the walk and eighteen of these were with companions. Several more days were in the company of stray fellow walkers met on the way, but I mostly walked alone.

For the first hour or so I was subdued at the thought of the enormity of the journey ahead, but soon I felt exhilarated and almost had to hold myself back from striding out too fast on the flat paths. The waymark for the GR5 was now becoming familiar – a horizontal white stripe over a red stripe. The French described this waymarking as *balisage*. Throughout my journey I was always on the lookout for these strips of paint. They might be found on poles, fences, on the ground, tree trunks, walls or boulders. Usually they were plentiful and easy to spot but sometimes they were maddeningly scarce or absent over whole stretches. It became a daily obsession to find the route but it was a joy to come back on course after an hour or more of confusion.

Following the first woodlands there was a long stretch along the Oranjedijk, on a straight asphalt path, and it was now getting warm. The great wide Waterweg appeared, with a procession of ships gliding along up to the port of Rotterdam, leaving v-shaped washes rolling on to the embankments. At the outskirts of Maasluis, a winding path with a lovely soft surface took us right into the old dock of the town.

To avoid the urban jungle of Rotterdam, laced with motorways, the route required that we take a ferry across the Waterweg where the trail began again in the little town of Rozenburg. Hillaby had no waymarked route to take him around the concrete conglomeration of this great Dutch city and his description of dodging the roaring traffic on a motorway intersection is hair-raising. We stopped at a café and sat on a sunny terrace: the first of many such respites to follow in the long hot summer to come. The route then threaded its way along and over a complex of waterways, starting with the Coalandkanaal. This is an engineered landscape of skeletal concrete and steel bridges, with ships improbably sailing through countryside. Over ruler-straight canals and intersecting roads with rivers of traffic, we could see our first night's destination – the ancient town of Brielle. We scrambled down a grassy embankment onto a peaceful path along the edge of the Brielse Meer, a waterway with pleasure craft and masses of water birds. I was dog-tired; my rucksack felt like a ton weight and my feet were burning from the continuous pounding on the hot, asphalt surfaces.

We entered through the gates of Brielle, crossing the moat and through the protective dyke with the brick bastions thrusting into the water. The hotel De Zalm was right in the centre and could not have come sooner.

That evening I was exhausted and my feet had monumental blisters. I was also very despondent about the next stage since my programme was to complete the section through Holland, to Bergen-Op-Zoom, in four days. Places to stay were also a problem since bed and breakfasts or hotels were few and far between; I had been warned about this in the tourist office at the Hook of Holland on the evening before I started. I was now almost overwhelmed by the immensity of the task I had set myself. Only 30km covered and over 2,200 still to go. It seemed impossible to me that first depressing night.

After some hard thinking, I decided to change my plan and add a day to the Dutch section. I felt better at once and went to bed early.

11 May

A beautiful morning, calm and mild, with blue sky appearing from the early cloud. Petra returned to Amsterdam and I set out strongly, enjoying the prospect of the easy day's stage ahead. The waymarks began again at the Gothic church in the centre of Brielle, an unfinished building which looked strange, almost as if it had been sliced in half. The route then led around the marvellous fortifications with their star-shaped, angled bastions, some with cannons pointing out towards the misty, flat and watery Dutch landscape.

Brielle is a famous town in the history of the Netherlands, associated with the uprising against the Spanish in 1572. The invaders had occupied the town in 1567 but some of the inhabitants managed to flee across the North Sea to Dover from where they planned a rebellion. The rebels, called the Watergeuzen, were again forced to leave and their fleet sailed for Germany. A sudden storm drove the ships back and the rebels recaptured their town. To the Dutch, this event marks the start of the liberation of the Netherlands.

Across the moat, the route first led me along the waterway called the Brielse Rak and then by the edge of the Oosterlandse Rak. For the first hour or so I walked alone, relishing the solitude, but then was overtaken by a large party of Dutch joggers. These were mostly women, dressed in multicoloured shorts and sweatshirts, but they were being marshalled along by a couple of fit-looking men. These specimens of good health, who were obviously leaders or coaches, leapt up and down, sprinted for a few metres, sometimes backwards, all the time keeping up a shouted commentary of orders to their unfortunate, sweating charges. I felt tired just looking at them.

When the route left the waterway, it led into an immense estate of little bungalows or more properly, 'wendy houses' which the Dutch use as weekend retreats. Most of these have tiny gardens and look like somewhat larger and more architectural versions of the allotment huts you see in England and Wales. They are so closely packed together, it is a wonder they can be seen as a means of getting away to the peace of the country. The Dutch are so used to living in densely populated cities and in tall apartment blocks that just being at ground level at weekends, close to their vegetables and flowers, must be their way of connecting with the earth.

I crossed under a big viaduct which takes the motorway out to Europort – just visible on the horizon as a fretwork of great oil tanks, chimneystacks and pylons, all softened and surreal in a purple heat haze. A path wound on to what was called on the map a *boulevarde*. Surprisingly, this turned out to be a narrow track alongside a wild and beautiful empty expanse of marsh and tall golden reed beds, full of birds. Dropping my rucksack, I flopped down on a bench, drinking in the peace and resting my burning feet which had been pounding hard surfaces practically every metre since I had left the beach. The writers of the Sierra Club guidebook to the GR5 had remarked that the flat walking in Holland was not to be assumed to be an easy effort. They were certainly right and the continuous hard surfaces and unchanging rhythm were cruel on my feet and leg muscles. I kept saying to myself that I would be all right after a week or so.

The weight of my rucksack was a problem. It was a shock for me to read that Hillaby had carried between 30 and 40 pounds on his epic trek, but I was even more discomfited to learn that he took long training walks with 50 pounds of cast iron discs sandwiched between the thick volumes of the London telephone directory! I had no desire to look like a walking rucksack and in any case I was, at 66, at least twenty years older than Hillaby when he had started his journey. When planning mine, I spent a long time deciding what was important and which items could be forsaken. Essentials like maps and guidebooks would have filled a rucksack alone. There were eleven guides for the whole route and innumerable maps. The best maps for walking were to a scale of 1:25,000 but if I took these for the whole route I would have needed a van, or a team of porters, to carry them. I had to settle for a scale of 1:50,000, which was just acceptable, and 1:100,000 which turned out to be almost useless. Even at these scales, there was an enormous bundle of maps and I had what I thought was the brilliant idea of cutting each map down to just the section I would walk on. Later, this turned out to be less than wise when I needed to go off the route to find a town with lodgings.

The weight of paper to be carried was considerably reduced by my reliance on supporters at different stages of the route.

Since the enterprise was to be undertaken throughout the summer, I took the chance of drastically limiting my clothes. A lightweight fleece jacket was to suffice for chilly days or nights – wool sweaters were out! A lightweight rainproof jacket turned out to be worse than useless, but in the end the problem was heat and drought rather than wetness. A small medical kit was essential and since I intended to make drawings to illustrate my journey, a sketchbook, a variety of pencils and a bottle of fixative built up the weight. An essential item for me was reading matter and a big question at an early stage was which book or books? I settled for the nine stories which made up Galsworthy's *The Forsyte Saga* which was available in three thick paperbacks. Volume one was to last me to Nancy in Lorraine; volume two as far as Lac Léman and the final book would take me across the Alps to the Mediterranean. I finally set out with just under twenty pounds which, for the first month or so, still felt too heavy.

Emulating Hillaby, I took a few training walks but without an overloaded rucksack. The most important of these was a nine day trek around the Kerry Way in the wild south-west of Ireland. Apart from getting fit, I learned a lot about clothes and equipment. I found that the boots I had planned to use were a disaster, leaving me with spectacular blisters after three days. Settling for wet feet, I finished the trail in light trainer-type shoes. These became my choice for the long walk and were largely a success. I brought two pairs and wore one pair out after 1,500km.

I came out on to a wide area of sand dunes on the tip of the island of Voourne with winding paths through stunted pines. Here I lost the route and eventually blundered out on to a suburban road. There was nobody about, so I walked on to find a sign or anything to tell me where I was since I was now obviously well off the map in my guide. Around a corner I spotted, to my relief, a VVV, Dutch Tourist Office, but, just like the café, this was closed. There was a large map outside and I was able to work out a route back to the GR. Coming into the village of Rockanje, I met my first serious walkers, complete with rucksacks. These were two middle-aged Dutch women who were walking the Holland section of the GR5 in the opposite direction, the variation which kept to the coast of Holland. It was reassuring to meet someone else in the pursuit of the same eccentric pleasures. After an exchange of stories I walked on with a stronger stride and a pack which felt slightly lighter. I would not meet another fellow walker for more than three weeks.

I had booked ahead into a bed and breakfast and arrived outside the neat suburban house in the late afternoon. An elderly woman opened the door but she could not speak English and seemed agitated at my sudden appearance. My Dutch was almost non-existent, but I recognised enough to understand that her daughter was the owner and was out until later in the evening. She allowed me sit on the shady patio and brought me a pot of tea. I saw my first swallows of the summer and after a huge Dutch dinner with lots of chips, a speciality of the Netherlands, went to bed early.

12 May

Sun and blue skies again. I savoured the prospect of a short day, with lots of rest to ease my sore feet: hoping I was learning to take each day as it came and not think about the immensity of the distance ahead. The official GR route wandered off behind the line of dunes, past acres of glasshouses, at the edge of the suburbs, and looked pretty boring. I decided to strike out directly for the sea about one kilometre through the broad band of sand dunes. Some of these were over four metres high and the land behind was just below sea level. As I crested the last high dune, the ocean was before me.

The tide was out and a wide stretch of sand led out to a shining sea. I had all day before me and only 13km to walk, so I decided on the luxury of lounging in the sunshine on the beach for a few hours. This being Holland, there was the freedom to go naked and when the day became hot it was a pleasure to make a few quick dashes into the icy waters of the North Sea. I felt better now that the journey was well started.

The cold North Sea: start of the GR5

The beach was nearly deserted at 10 a.m., but since it was a national holiday in the Netherlands it did not take long for people to drift out of the dunes and settle down into little groups on the beach. After a pleasant few hours I reluctantly hoisted my rucksack and set off across the wide sands towards the distant great dam and sluices: the Haringvlietdam and the Haringvlietsluizen.

Three great rivers of Europe converge at this point to form the delta of south-west Holland. The grandest of these is the Rhine which, fed by waters from the northern slopes of the Swiss Alps, flows 1,300km to the sea. The Maas starts life as the Meuse in eastern France, while the Scheldt journeys 430km from northern France. These rivers create a bewildering lacework of waterways when they reach the lowlands. When it crosses the Dutch frontier, the Ijssel splits from the Rhine and then flows north into the former Zuider Zee. The Rhine itself becomes the Waal and is joined by the Maas, splitting again into dozens of waterways to form the delta.

On the night of 31 January 1953 the vast cluster of islands which formed the delta was battered by a ferocious storm. The protective dykes which surrounded the low-lying land gave way and the sea poured in over huge areas of land. More than 1,800 people died, overwhelmed by the waters. The islands all but disappeared and the inundation spread far inland.

The Dutch, who had lived with this apocalyptic prospect for centuries, responded in characteristically robust fashion. The Delta Plan, prepared for such a catastrophe, began three years later and over the next 30 years a stupendous engineering achievement finally tamed the waters. The separate, vulnerable islands of the delta were stitched together by an astonishing network of canals, dams, bridges, dykes, sluices and barrages.

The line of outer dams protects against the ocean and creates huge inland lakes. These are used for fresh water supply, as well as recreation, for one of the most densely populated countries in the world. A further line of secondary dams, near the multiple mouths of the rivers, controls flood waters and all the dams and barrages carry roads on top which link into an intricate system of motorways. I was soon to plunge into this new tectonic landscape.

Walking on the damp sand was sheer pleasure after the hard surfaces of the paths. More and more people appeared, stripped for the sun and sea and largely ignoring the solitary walker with the rucksack.

The huge bulk of the dam loomed in front and, as I left the beach, the red and white sign of the GR reappeared and led me on to it. The structure was almost 4km straight across, with the sea on one side and the great inland lake of the Haringvliet on the other. Two lanes of fast and continuous traffic flowed along the top of the dam but there was also a narrow concrete service road, free of cars, and I plodded along this, counting off the sixteen concrete and steel sluices.

On the other side of the dam, the route turned sharp right, past the Stellendamhaven, filled with smart boats, and led out onto an area of scrub-covered dunes. I lay down to rest my hot and blistered feet. The hard surface of the dam had not improved matters. It was restful to lie in the long grass at the top of a bank and watch kestrels working the canopy of dwarf shrubbery below me. Cuckoos called and there was birdsong everywhere. The sun got far too hot for lying down so I reluctantly set off again. The path ahead was hard-surfaced and I hobbled along with fiery soles until I got into my own rhythm and stride, all the time watching out for aggressive Dutch racing cyclists tearing along the paths shared with the walkers. It appeared that the mad cyclists have the right of way. Although this was supposedly my precious 'short' day, the last few kilometres seemed unending.

The village of Goedereede, with its squat church tower, appeared and on its outskirts, the modern motel where I had reserved a room. I reached the halfway point of my route through Holland at Goodereede, the pronunciation of which was almost as difficult as the famous Scheveningen – a sort of rattle at the back of the upper palate. I had walked only 60km, but needed to give myself some encouragement at this juncture. Daily targets, hours walked, kilometres in an hour, minutes per kilometre, how long to reach that distant landmark could become an obsession.

The GR turns east here and follows the shore of another new inland waterway, Grevelingen, and then along the canalised river Scheldt, before finally leaving the North Sea far behind. The motel was surprisingly full of people, but I realised at dinner that they were mainly Dutch, having a meal after the holiday: few guests were staying overnight. The manager told me about two Canadian walkers, Charlotte and Sven, who were ahead of me and going all the way to Nice. I first heard about them in the Hook of Holland, where they had stayed at the same bed and breakfast as me and were seven days in front. I wondered if I would ever catch up with them and if so where. While I was sitting alone in the cheerful dining room, with animated talk in Dutch all around me, I was confronted with the loneliness of the solitary long-distance walker. A half bottle of wine helped, followed by a bath and bed.

13 May
I felt wonderful after a comfortable night's sleep. I took a needle to my huge blisters, drained and dressed them and felt I was good for a few more stages.

At breakfast I was seated near a table of three men: two English, with North Country accents, and one Dutchman. The conversation was all about getting Mercedes cars into Britain and the necessity for respraying them. I speculated as to whether I was listening in to a genuine business conversation or if murky deals were being done.

The early morning was again splendid: wide blue skies and a cool wind. As I left the hotel, I turned east towards the mainland of Holland. For most of the marvellous day that followed, I met hardly anyone, I saw no cars; even the noise of traffic, constant in Holland so far, had disappeared.

I was now finally turning my back on the North Sea. The hinterland of Europe lay ahead. An hour's walk on an empty straight road, across a table-flat geometrical landscape had me lost in thought, something that would occupy me more and more and I found myself increasingly slipping into daydreaming in the solitary months ahead.

In 1950, I had set out on a similar journey across Europe. I was 22 and a student of architecture. This was my first visit to mainland Europe and just five years after Second World War, travel was becoming possible. My plan was to cycle to Rome and back, a sort of plebeian version of the Grand Tour. In the tradition of students of architecture, I carried a sketchbook along with my Brownie box-camera. Landing at Dieppe in the middle of August, I rode to Paris via a bombed-out Rouen. Paris was an enchanting place to me then, although, as an impoverished student, my only experience of French cuisine was from an army steel ration tray in a camp site near the Rodin Museum. The road to the south-east, although a *Route Nationale*, was quiet in those days and my memory is of huge distances covered along straight roads lined with tall poplars.

Past Vesoul and Troyes, I went through the Gap of Belfort and into Switzerland, to be amazed by the cleanliness, order and obvious wealth of that country after the shortages and economy of the war years. Everywhere in France there were signs of destruction: smashed bridges, ruined buildings and walls pockmarked by shells and bullets. Lake Lucerne was an intense blue and the first sight of the Alps enrolled me as a would-be mountaineer for life. I remembered my shortness of breath on the summit of the St Gotthard Pass, the chill of the high altitude air on the summit and then the sheer exhilaration of the 50-km downhill dash to Lake Como, swooping around bends on largely empty, beautifully engineered roads.

A combination of boredom and exhaustion, following day after day of punishing pedalling, made me give up in Milan. The great Galleria and the spiky marble pinnacles of the Gothic cathedral were wonders to an aspiring architect. The temptations of a slow train and a very cheap ticket took bicycle and me to Rome. I stopped off in Florence to experience the architecture and made a drawing of the Ponte Vecchio, the only intact bridge left over the Arno: all of the others were destroyed by the retreating Germans. Student beggars and pavement artists were common then and I tried my luck with my hat on the path as I made my drawing. The miserable few liras thrown in did not take me very far. In the centre of Rome, having little money left, I queued at a centre for pilgrims and was rewarded with free accommodation and basic meals for a week, way out on the Via Aurelia in a concrete, Fascist-style apartment block.

The return journey was a lesson in survival. I had very little money and crawled along the Mediterranean, lodging and eating when I could in monasteries, Salvation Army hostels; sleeping on the beach and surreptitiously eating grapes and digging potatoes from the edges of fields. It was the end of the summer; the youth hostels were nearly empty, and the kitchen shelves held opened packets of unfinished food, particularly a kind of porridge oats. This free food kept me alive. Monte Carlo, Nice, Cannes, St Tropez all slipped past until Marseilles gave me the opportunity to see Le Corbusier's famous and newly built *Unité Habitation.*

The long haul up the Rhône valley in a half-starved state remains a blur of sensations; eating a gift of slabs of nougat in Montélimar; being fed by two kindly Australian women tourists near Avignon and a filthy but free Communist-run hostel of the *Amis de la Nature,* near Vienne. As I left the town of Mâcon, I entered an area of vineyards and when I tentatively appeared at an ancient farmhouse I was given a job picking grapes. The division of labour was marked in those days. The men carried the large wicker baskets from the pickers and brought them to the carts for transport back to the vats. The women were the pickers and since I was considered raw, I was put with them to pluck the bunches of grapes and fill the baskets. At 6 p.m. the work ended and the women went to the farmhouse while the men emptied the grapes into a huge vat. Then we all sampled earlier vintages from small glasses before sitting down to the evening meal. The wine was plentiful, a dozen bottles or more on the table, and since my bed was in an attic over the barn, I had to crawl up the steps every night.

My pay was minuscule but the food saved my life and the few francs lasted to Paris. An all-night bike ride led to my falling off several times with sleep. I ended up lying in a haycock and waking with frost on the grass and then ate apples from roadside trees in Normandy until the final downhill stretch to the port in Dieppe welcomed. From Newhaven and

Brighton to London and then on the train and ship at Holyhead, I subsisted on a little saved chocolate and apples gathered into my cycle panniers. Arriving home in the middle of October, I was chided by the professor for turning up late for the start of term. That had been more than half a lifetime ago.

I was now striding out on a new journey after a night in a soft bed and a good breakfast, credit cards in my wallet, but old memories came back: the wind in my face as I sped along on the gold Raleigh 'Kestrel'; the smell of Gauloises; coffee and early morning baguettes; ripe peaches and *vin ordinaire* in my aluminium water bottle fixed to the bike, sucked up through a rubber tube.

I got a rude awakening when the road ended and there was no obvious way forward. The guidebook clearly showed the route going out onto the wide marsh but a wall of impenetrable vegetation barred the way. The *Wandelpad 5–1* had bifurcated at Goedereede and the route had been clearly marked until then. It began to look as if the coastal path was the most used option and that the inland section, the start of the GR5 proper, was not so popular. I had a slight sense of foreboding since I had no idea if the GR5 was a well-walked route. The only thing I had heard was that the Alpine section was a well-known trek. This, however, was months away. The excellent Sierra Club guidebook to the route by Susanna Margolis and Ginger Harmon was of enormous help when planning stages but already this next section of the way had changed from their ten-year-old description.

A closer study of the map in the Dutch guidebook revealed a dotted line inland of the marsh and I guessed that this might be an indication of an alternative route if the water level was higher. Struggling along this for a kilometre or so produced an escape route through ragged bushes out onto the wide sweep of the marsh.

This wilderness was about 6km long and was called the Slikken van Flakkee. The route here was unmarked except for the occasional small pole, but the way was obvious: straight ahead. I had translated a few essential key words: *rechtsaf*, turn right; *linksaf*, turn left; *oversteken*, cross over; *volgen*, follow. The fact that a walking path was *Wandelpad* and not *Fietspad*, which is for cycles, was why some cyclists had shouted at me.

The sky was clear and cobalt blue. For the first time on the walk I wanted to emulate Hazlitt:

> *Give me the clear blue sky over my head, and the green turf beneath my feet, a winding road before me, and a three hours walk to dinner and then to thinking! It is hard if I cannot start some game on these lone heaths. I laugh, I run, I leap, I sing for joy.*

Diederikse Zeedijk, Holland

The turf was decidedly wet and the track as straight as an arrow. I had at least six hours to dinner but the lone heath was beautiful: wild scrub, loud with birdsong and the springy softness of the track made me also sing for joy. There were no sounds except those of nature, and the flat landscape seemed immense with the distant waters of the inland Grevelingen gleaming to the south.

After 9km of this blissful walking, I came out onto a hard road around the Polder Roxen, but within a few minutes the route climbed up to the top of a long grassy dyke, lined with trees on the land side and speckled with yellow buttercups. This great green highway, the Diederikse Zeedijk, stretched to the horizon, a Vauban-like fortification against the forces of the sea and floods. Halfway along I saw a couple of men working in a field below the dyke. One of them waved and shouted in Dutch, which I understood to mean 'Where are you going?' 'To Nice' I shouted back and they punched their fists to the sky. Buoyed by the encounter and by the superb day, I covered another 5km before flopping down in the grass for lunch.

When I started again, I was stiff and going more slowly. The dyke now curved right around and I had my first view of my destination – the huge Grevelingendam lying low across the far distance. Two boys were flying kites in the stiff breeze now coming in off the water. At this point the dyke was nearly 6m high and the map showed that the land inside was as low as 0.01m. I imagined the storm of that January night in 1953. The day was getting hot and the water's edge was now at the bottom of the dyke and looked tempting. I found a tiny shingle spit poking out from the sharp rocks and enjoyed what was to be my last dip in the (at least partly saline) water until the Mediterranean.

The GR marker: on the way to Grevelingendam

The grass route and the solitude ended abruptly at the harbour of Herkingen where hundreds of young windsurfers scooted in every direction in an explosion of colours and a powerful wind. It was a straight 5km walk to the dam on a new, wide dyke of blindingly white tarmac. This was a hard walk; it seemed endless, with the great dam only slowly growing bigger in front of me. The dyke was lined with huge wind turbines, each on a single metal stalk; I counted these off with the monotonous soughing of the great blades rising and falling as I passed.

The traffic over the dam was heavy and I had to wait for an age before a gap allowed me to sprint across. I had 3km of road-walking to get to the tiny village of Oude Tonge. This was off my route unfortunately but necessary to find a bed for the night. The bed and breakfast was pleasant enough, providing a necessary beer, a large meal and an early bed. I had been out eight hours and was weary. I was happy with my 27km walked that day, though felt that it would take me about ten days to get really fit and to enjoy each day fully.

14 May

I found a taxi to take me back the 3km to the start of the trail at the dam. This made me feel better at the beginning of a day that was to be a relentlessly hard walk on tarmac and concrete: a way which snaked through a technological landscape of concrete dam structures and above all roads, roads and more roads and an endless flow of cars and trucks. For all that, it was lonely, without the pleasure of solitude of a natural landscape. I felt isolated from the thousands in their sealed metal boxes tearing past. The only consolation was the fact that I could walk on an empty secondary way, parallel to the main road and along the waterway or occasional marshland filled with huge flocks of birds: oystercatchers, duck, sandpipers, curlews, plover and hundreds of grazing geese.

The Grevelingendam leads straight on to the Philipsdam, which is a far greater enterprise – almost 6km long and formed in a sinuous treble curve. The complicated system of sluices, harbours and ship locks contrasted with the peaceful marshland of the previous day. I left the horrible roaring highway as a GR sign led me down an empty little roadway to the banks of the Shelde-Rijn canal, which leads from Antwerp and on into Belgium. The route follows the wide waterway for a long stretch and there was a regular procession of enormous barges steadily forging by, their engines hypnotically thudding.

The great canal curved away to the flat horizon, and an

elegant bow-shaped bridge was a distant landmark to be reached. Bridges, water towers, church steeples, tall chimneys – these were to become my beacons during the days of flat country walking ahead. This was also a horticultural landscape: an intensely managed one with vast billowing sheets of glistening plastic and young green new potatoes beginning to poke through. I could see the bridge from over 6km away, and an hour and a half later I walked on to it.

An old Dutch windmill was an indication that I was at last leaving the man-made polders of the delta. This was one day I was not enjoying, I decided as I stopped on the bridge to eat lunch. The route led me over the bridge to the opposite bank but, irritatingly, instead of following the opposite side of the waterway, it made a long detour into the village of Nieuw-Vossemeer before turning back to the banks. There was a welcome café attached to a recreation ground and, surprisingly, it seemed to be entirely German-speaking. I found out later that this part of Holland is favoured by Germans from the west of the country since it is only a few hours away by motorway. I went back on to a footpath along the waterway and eventually, after a punishing seven hours of blistering heat and hard pavement, I came into the town of Halsteren. This was only a short distance from Bergen-op-Zoom where I was to meet Petra at noon the next day. I could go no farther, however, and felt I had reached a low point in morale.

An old-fashioned hotel by the roadside beckoned and I checked in but felt too exhausted to eat. I despaired about completing this journey if I could feel so bad after only five days and just over 100km. Lying on the bed in a darkened room, I thought of earlier, successful, long mountain walks and climbs: a fifteen-hour day in the Dauphine Alps with Nuala when we had to climb a second mountain pass since there was nowhere to stay after the first steep climb; eight hours through the magnificent Granite Canyon in Wyoming; an endless day up into the Sierra Nevada in California to camp at Graveyard Lakes; the lung-bursting climb to the top of the Freshfield Pass in the Ruwenzorí Mountains in the centre of Africa, or a lifetime of long walks on the hills and mountains of Ireland.

What was wrong with me? I had walked entirely on the flat for five days. Was I getting too old for this sort of stuff? The answer may have been in the comments by the Sierra guide: that walking continuously on flat surfaces imposes special strains. The writers' opinion was that flat walking for long periods is physically tiring because the same sets of muscles are used. It is mentally tiring because of the flat horizons. The hard surfaces I knew all about since my feet were now raw.

15 May

It rained in the night. The morning was cool and I felt better. The hotel would not serve me breakfast until 9 a.m., possibly because it was Sunday, so I set off late. After the hard surfaces of the previous day, I had the luxury of soft woodland paths and grassy farm tracks. Later I met joggers, walkers and more of the demon Dutch cyclists who constantly demanded the right of way everywhere. I went badly wrong after an hour; entirely my own fault since I was not looking out properly for the small red-and-white markers and just plodded on along what looked like an obvious track. Rule one of the long distance trail walker's code then applied: if you have not seen a marker for fifteen minutes or so, you are probably walking the wrong way! Depressing though it may be, you *must* retrace your steps to where you spotted the last sign. This was to be the first of many such backtracking exercises. Returning, I carefully looked out for the point where I had seen the last marker. Once I spotted the familiar sign, a careful reconaissance located another marker on the side of a tree and the route revealed itself as a narrow track which wound around the ruins of the star-shaped fort, Fort De Rover, one of several which had defended the old town of Bergen-op-Zoom.

The early part of the walk led through pleasant deciduous woods before opening out to straight tracks that led past miles of intensive horticultural landscape.

By midday I was walking along the railway line into the old centre of the town. Petra had arranged to meet me at the railway station and walk with me for two days into Belgium. I was glad to see that she was already in the café and I flopped down for a cool drink and an hour's rest. The plan had been to continue to Essen on the Belgian border that afternoon, but I was much too tired and dispirited by my lack of fitness. I decided to rest there for the remainder of the day and tomorrow make for Kalmthout – in Flanders. Petra was full of energy and was very disappointed not to push on at once. I felt that it was I who should have been fighting fit. She, too, had blisters after that long first day but was much more accepting of them than me; a further reason for feeling bad. Petra gave in to my temporary defeatism and we took a long lunch in the sunshine, sitting on a terrace outside a café in the Grote Markt of the old town. In the afternoon I felt energetic enough to do a drawing and this further improved my morale.

I usually bring a sketchbook with me on my trips and even though a camera is an easier option, particularly for recording buildings, I feel unfulfilled if I do not return with at least one drawing. I still had the sketchbook from my student trip and

Grote Markt, Bergen-op-Zoom

resolved to continue the tradition. In the early twentieth century Le Corbusier filled a sketchbook on his Italian tour and Raymond McGrath, another pioneer of modern architecture and one of the most prolific and remarkable draughtsmen of all, produced hundreds of watercolour, ink and pencil sketches on his many journeys through Europe.

I must confess that the weight of a camera was also a deciding factor but on my way through the duty-free at Heathrow I had given in to the temptation of one of the lightweight automatics, judging it to be a lot less problematic than my heavy Nikon. The real joy for me, however, was drawing in soft pencil on a crisp, slightly textured cartridge paper. When a drawing is going well, the sensual pleasure of using a 7B to create shapes and shadows is hard to beat.

The map of the town was intriguing: a dense cluster of concentric streets and lanes – a truly medieval enclosure, with the town wall missing. This had been demolished in the late nineteenth century and only the pattern of the outer circular street marks its path. Like Brielle, my first night's stop, this old town was also famous for withstanding a Spanish siege in the sixteenth century. The Markienzenhof, the court of the Marquis, dates from the early sixteenth century and is now a museum. St Geertruidskerk and the Raadhuis – a typical Dutch town hall – are other old buildings, evocative of the past sturdy individualism of Holland.

That evening I reviewed my progress. It did not look very impressive – six days to complete the Dutch section of the GR5 and only 122km covered. I went to bed early in a gloomy mood. Even the racy, Amsterdam-style, redbrick hotel failed to interest me. Picking at my blistered feet looked like becoming my latest obsession.

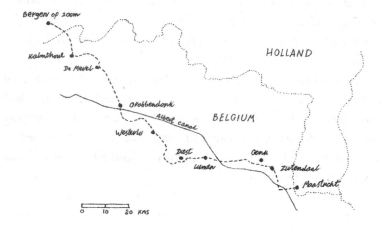

Map 3: Flanders

40

CHAPTER 2

Across Flanders Fields

16 May

I was to cross into Belgium today. This was progress. A glance at the map of the whole route, however, was more sobering. I was now leaving the North Sea, having seemingly traversed only a jumble of islands off the coast of Holland.

The morning was cool and overcast and I felt rejuvenated after the depression of the day before. The *Jeugdberberg,* youth hostel, was a couple of kilometres outside the town and it was here that the GR5 began before the extension to the open sea at the Hook of Holland. There are suggestions that it will be further extended to cross England from the Irish Sea, perhaps the famous Wainwright coast to coast route. What then but a logical coast-to-coast route across Ireland from County Donegal to the Mourne Mountains, making it an Atlantic Ocean to the Mediterranean trail.

Such was my enthusiasm and fantasy that morning.

A wooden signpost outside the building pointed south, with *Riviera* in prominent white letters. I felt that I was now really on my way and couldn't wait to set off. The hostel provided us with the address of a bed and breakfast in Kalmthout and this was encouraging since I was now heading into territory where lodgings were scarce. The sun came out and the day got hotter, but all the early section was in woods, on lovely soft, sandy paths through pines mixed with glorious fresh green oaks. A long shaded track led past fields straight to the Belgian frontier, marked by a tiny stone bridge and a modest sign. This was the first border of many I was to cross in the New Europe, non-guarded, shuttered frontier posts without passport controls.

The path went along the frontier to the quiet little town of Essen and detoured around the old estate of Kiekenhove where we reached the first café – it was closed on Mondays. A kilometre farther on there was another and we enjoyed a filter coffee in the sunshine. Then it was back into the woods for a long stretch. Here I found the first mosquitoes of the season, or rather they found me. I had unfortunately changed into shorts and quickly changed back to long pants but it was too late and I was bitten savagely. My insect repellent was firmly packed away in the bottom of my rucksack for the later summer since I had not expected the pests so soon.

An early shock was the change from the Dutch guide to the new Belgian guide for the long trail across Flanders. The precisely detailed, large-scale maps of the earlier stretches made route-finding easy, even when the markers were scarce. The new guide had maps of half the scale, so care was needed to watch for bends in the track or woods where there were dozens of other paths.

The sun was high when we started across the glorious Kalmthoutse Heide nature reserve. This is a wide stretch of heathland with sand dunes, pines and silver birch, all alive with birdsong. Soft sand made the trail difficult. With the heat at the end of a long day, we were now ready to call a halt. We eventually came out on to the busy N111 and looked for No 5, our prospective lodging. The first number we saw was 177. On along the straight tarmac ribbon to Kalmthout, with no footpath and speeding traffic, thirsty and exhausted, we at last knocked on the door of No 5. The woman who opened the door looked perplexed when we asked for rooms. It turned out that the number was a mistake; it should have been 51, the hotel we had passed halfway back. She saw our disappointment and invited us in for a glass of water. As we relaxed on a newly built wooden deck at the rear of the house, we felt enormously better.

Mady Bouckaert's husband, Jacques, joined us from the garden and iced fruit juice and then tea soon followed the jugs of water. The couple were intrigued by my plans and were enthusiastic about introducing us to friends of theirs who were also interested in walking for pleasure. They phoned the hotel to reserve places and, after showers, took us out to dinner in a nearby restaurant. I drank my first Belgian beer – a *Duvel,* chosen from the bewildering list of varieties and followed by an excellent meal. The friends joined us later; one of these, a sprightly 80-year-old, was the walking enthusiast. He was a freelance journalist who had founded a 'men only' club many years before to engage in what he called 'stress-free walking'. The women in the party raised their eyes to heaven at his rationalisation of their exclusion.

That night I felt totally spent and after seven days of effort decided that a full day of rest was essential if I was to restore my body for the long way ahead. Later there was a spectacular storm with heavy rain accompanied by thunder and lightning. I hoped that this would take away the leaden heat.

We had clocked up 30km that day – the same as day one, so I suppose I had a right to be tired but I was still dispirited about my continuously sore feet.

Kalmthoutse Heide, Belgium

17 May
This was definitely a day for recuperation. After we had a leisurely breakfast, the hotel, which had been empty the night before, now seemed crowded with people, mainly elderly. They were being ushered into a large conference room where a loud-voiced man appeared to be delivering a sales pitch. Petra explained that this was a common event in the Netherlands where groups of people, and it mainly appealed to the retired, were taken on coach trips into the countryside where they were given basic meals and then subjected to sales talk for all sorts of household goods. In this case the product was blankets. She said that most people went for the excursion and the meal and

tried to resist buying anything. I was to experience such events at several hotels on my way south.

I strolled out on to the *Kalmthoutse Heide* which now felt fresh and cool. It was a real pleasure to walk slowly with no rucksack and no target destination. I sat on a grassy bank and spent a quiet few hours drawing. It was peaceful on the wide heath except for an occasional twitter of birdsong. Later, a few hours spent sitting out on a café terrace drinking beer all helped to renew my energy and willpower and even the awful evening meal in the same café did not spoil a rewarding rest day. The truly terrible meal included being charged the equivalent of £1 for each glass of tap water and when the waiter offered more *frites*, he added them to the bill. He was dismissive when challenged about this and when we asked to see the manager he said *he* was the boss. This was not the sole bad meal I was to have during that long summer but it was the only experience of rude behaviour by staff.

Rest days were perfect for daydreaming but also offered the opportunity for long spells of reading. The fat first volume of *The Forsyte Saga* was a pleasure and Galsworthy's gentle but ironic mockery of the Forsyte values a perfect antidote to the rigours of my long journey.

18 May

Petra returned to Amsterdam after walking about an hour or so towards the village of Wurestwezel. It was a fresh beautiful morning after yet another night of heavy rain. I felt great after the rest and strode along strongly. It was a dull walk, however, in the early stages at least, mostly along hard roads; it was relentlessy suburban, being the outskirts of Antwerp. This was guard dog territory and the morning walk was through a cacophony of barks and snarls. At one point the way went down a narrow path with one savage monster leaping to the top of the fence all along its territory. Signs outside most houses had a picture of the resident mutt with the warning message '*Ik Waak hier*' ('I'm watching here'). From the few inhabitants I saw, there were not many greetings. During the next week or so through this part of Flanders, I developed a hatred for suburbia.

A section of road led through the middle of a military zone with signs on both sides forbidding entry, while loud bangs of artillery were a reminder of the Great War and that I was walking through the fields of Flanders. I thought of my Uncle Joe, my mother's favourite brother.

Joseph Gaffney ran away from home at the age of sixteen to join the British Army. His romantic ideal of war was the cavalry regiment with its pennants, lances and fancy uniforms. Boys' books of the time were full of stories of the charge of the Light Brigade, the North-West Frontier and tales of heroic sacrifice; nothing of death and mutilation, boredom and horror. My Uncle Joe's choice of regiment was the Eighth Royal Irish Hussars and after enlisting he was promptly shipped to India. This was early 1914.

That August the massive German army swept across this part of Flanders. The Schlieffen Plan was designed to encircle Paris by attacking through what Von Clausewitz called the 'stomach of France'. Uncle Joe's regiment was sent back at once to the Western Front. He was given no horse, plumed helmet or lance but had to trudge through the mud of Flanders in a khaki uniform and steel helmet with a rifle and bayonet. He was still only sixteen when he was in the demoralising retreat from Mons and, soon after, through his older brother, who was also in the army, his parents managed to get him discharged as being under age.

Joe did not give up, though, and shortly afterwards he was off again, this time to sea with the Merchant Navy. He qualified as one of the early Marconi radio ships' officers and for about fifteen years circumnavigated the globe several times in tramp steamers. A fragment of one of his diaries survives and is full of terse entries detailing ports called at, next destinations and miles sailed. His romantic soul can be guessed at from the bald list of exotic places: Yokohama, Shanghai, Seattle, Panama, Buenos Aires, Suez, Sydney, San Francisco, Valletta.

Joe developed tuberculosis and died in 1930, aged 32. I never met him but his memory was preserved in the family and my mother often told me the stories of his travels.

The Western Front and its terrible killing grounds lasted for four years on a more or less static line to the west of my route. On the way south I was to encounter many reminders of this conflict and the Second World War.

The village of Brecht had an apparently pointless detour into the centre where everything was closed, including the tourist office – on a Wednesday. Earlier the closing day had been Monday. I had chanced on only one open tourist office since the start. Earlier I had been told there was a hotel, De Merel, some 5 or 6km off the GR and I studied the map in the guidebook to plot a route. Unfortunately the actual place was off the map, so I had to rely on the directions I was given. The noise of a motorway, parallel to my direction and a kilometre or so to the west, acted as a sort of handrail. Along the way every house was shuttered and nobody answered my knock until I had reached the outskirts of a large wood. Here, at one isolated house, a woman gave me directions to De Merel.

The previous night's rain had left large puddles on the rough forest track, and mosquitoes were breeding in millions.

I tried to give these a wide berth, but still got bitten. The sprawling hotel buildings appeared eventually in a wide clearing. It turned out that I was the only guest in this somewhat spartan place which seemed to cater for weekend sports. The iron-framed narrow beds were not designed for luxury and the bathrooms were down a long corridor and seemed designed more for gymnasium ablutions. It was inexpensive, however, and the food was good. I phoned my granddaughter on her second birthday!

19 May

I headed due east on a map bearing to strike the Kempen Canal. When I reached the canal bank, the only bridge in sight was far to the north and to the south the view of water dissolved into a distant misty blur. Tantalisingly, I could see the GR markings on the far side. I was tempted to strip off and swim the 30m or so wide canal. What to do with my rucksack was the problem. I thought of all those survival courses and problem-solving by lateral thinking. Tie it to a log and tow it over? I walked off north, seeing the bridge growing larger but far too slowly. Every time the route took me off my longed-for due south direction was a major irritation, leaving me with a slow-burning resentment. The daily rhythms of long-distance walking were developing automatic responses to events on the trail – a reflection of life: elation, disappointment, resentment, euphoria, travail and repose.

I passed over Brugll and back down the canal, then set off inland, zigzagging on minor roads and farm tracks. It was a wonderfully peaceful walk with the singing of blackbirds, warblers, skylarks and only the distant sound of motorway traffic. Two huge black forms flashed over me and a shuddering blast of jet engines destroyed the tranquillity. These were only the first of many encounters with low-flying fighters over the weeks to come. Calm returned and a peaceful path through woods led past a Trappist monastery. This was a beautiful place with an avenue of chestnut trees and the ground white with fallen blossom.

It was a strange experience crossing, by footbridge, a big motorway. The traffic roar vanished in minutes in the woods on the other side.

I was walking fast for the first time and covered 15km in an amazingly short time. The second half of the day's stage was slower and a definite pattern was forming, with speedy and highly confident starts and gradual slowing after the first four hours. It was just over 30km into the small town of Grobbendonk and I strode into the centre still full of beans. There was a pleasant, new-looking hotel right in front of me. The door was locked and nobody answered the bell. At the bar-café next door, the barman shrugged and said that the hotel was closed. I went outside and followed signs to the local tourist office which led me out on to the banks of the Albert Canal. The signs vanished after a kilometre or so. I was baffled. A tourist office could not be located in such a bleak area and I was now footsore. I cursed the local tourist people and since it was now after 4.30, the office was likely to be closed. Back in the town centre, I ordered a cool beer in the bar-café and asked the barman to phone for a taxi.

The driver suggested the nearby larger town of Herentals, also on the banks of the Albert Canal, and after a short ride he deposited me outside what looked like a modest hotel. It wasn't. The rate for bed and breakfast was at city prices and since all my overnights so far in Holland and Belgium were well above budget, I hoped that the later stages would leave my overdraft looking healthier.

The hotel room was comfortable, however, and a good bath soothed my temper. I had no appetite and even less when the meal I ordered in the nearest restaurant arrived at my table. The menu was one of those where the meals are featured in glossy-coloured photographs. Mine tasted as if it was the actual one photographed. I toyed with the food and went back to bed and watched Belgian TV – an idiotic game show – before falling asleep.

20 May
The hotel was located above a beauty parlour. The elegant staff also managed the hotel and served breakfast. The only other people staying were a couple of business types – on expense accounts I sourly surmised. I wondered about the scarcity of places to stay. No bed and breakfast houses – the last one was six days back – and few hotels on the route. The only explanation I could think of was that Holland and Belgium are so small that people prefer to sleep at home. I remember telling a group of students at the University of Nebraska that if Nebraska had the population density of Holland, it would contain the entire population of the USA.

Mirabile dictu, I found the local tourist office open. Three cheers and, even better, a charming and helpful young woman booked me into places all the way to Maastricht. A bus took me back to the GR at the bridge over the Albert Canal at Grobendonk. After the storming performance of the day before, legs were aching and my feet were sore. I had given myself ten days to settle in and now on the eleventh I was as bad as ever. In this gloomy mood I hobbled on past farms, through woods on nice paths, but the agony of my feet spoiled it. According to the map in the guidebook, the route was now pointing in a general south-easterly direction but it weaved erratically to avoid main roads, seeking quiet laneways. The flat walking and relentless hard surfaces were becoming exceedingly boring and the horizon was now rarely more than a few 100m away and defined by a stand of trees or a near view of village rooftops.

In quick succession the villages of Bouwel, Herenthout and Noorderwijk were bypassed, through fields, along avenues of fresh green beeches and chestnut trees, when suddenly the walls of the great Norbertine Abbey of Tongerloo appeared ahead. The Norbertijnerabdij was founded in 1130 but the present buildings date from 1479, with further extensions in 1618. The Abbey houses a remarkable copy of Leonardo da Vinci's 'The Last Supper', possibly the work of one of the master's pupils. When I saw the original of this work in Milan, it was extraordinary to realise how near the masterpiece had come to obliteration in the Second World War when a direct hit by Allied bombing demolished the little church which housed it and only the wall with the da Vinci work survived intact. The next day the Milanese frantically erected temporary roofing and saved one of the treasures of Western art.

I limped into the small town of Westerloo and continued to the Centrum. I asked several passers-by where the Hotel Ars Valendi was but nobody had heard of it. Another bar-café provided the answer and I was informed that it was miles out in the countryside and way off my route; in fact more or less back the way I had just come! The Sierra guide authors were certainly right about the problems of overnight accommodation in the Lowlands.

I repeated my strategy of the day before: order a cold beer and ask the barperson to phone for a taxi. While there is huge pleasure in setting out for a long day's walk, there is nothing more disquieting than the possibility of no inn at the road's end.

Settling into the taxi, I fantasied about an old country inn with a civilised meal, followed by a quiet sleep. The reality was what looked like a vast truck parking lot in front of the banal brick wall of a supermarket. The first difficulty was to find someone to check me in since there appeared to be no reception desk. Eventually I found someone to show me to my room. The 'hotel' turned out to be, effectively, a linear attachment to a huge sports hall. I appeared to be the only guest and my room had no towels, soap or toilet paper. Back to the so-called reception where I was told that I must wait for the owner, who would be back at 8 p.m. I was now hungry as well as exhausted and was directed to a nearby restaurant where I was told that the owner would join me as soon as possible. A reasonable meal and a few glasses of wine later, my temper was slowly improving when a young man sat down opposite me and introduced himself as the hotel proprietor. A genial character with a plausible manner, he assured me that all my problems would be solved. When I told him about my long diversion from the route of the GR, he immediately offered to drive me back to the start of the next stage in the morning. A combination of more wine and this assurance sent me to bed in reasonable spirits.

Loud shouts and sounds of footballs being kicked in the corridor kept me awake for several hours and, although the usual ten pages of *Forsyte* helped, I took a long time to drift off.

21 May
After breakfast I went to meet the owner at the appointed place and time. There was no sign of him. I waited and waited in the empty car park, surrounded by locked doors and shuttered

windows. It was like the end of the world or maybe just Sunday in Belgium! Searching around desperately, I heard sounds behind the door of a closed café and managed to locate a cleaning lady who offered to phone my 'host'.

Twenty minutes later he roared up in a new car, casually dressed in a tracksuit. My bill for the bed and breakfast was 1,300 francs which I thought was far too much for what was just hostel standard. However, he cheerfully drove me all the way back to the GR at the point where I had finished the day before and for this I was truly grateful.

Crossing a bridge, the route led into the estate of Kasteel de Merode, a Renaissance castle standing at the water's edge with high-pitched roofs and spiky turrets. My path wound along the banks of the river and then dramatically turned into a magnificent avenue of giant plane trees. The ground was soft and springy, diagonal shafts of sunlight stabbed across the trail and purple rhododendron bloomed between the tree trunks. This was a wonderful quiet walk for an hour or two, with only a couple of cyclists to break the solitude. The hard-surfaced roads soon returned and I reached the halfway point of the day's stage at the little town of Averbode. The Abdji van Averbode is another great Norbertine foundation of 1134 and has become a popular retreat and pilgrimage centre. When I stepped out from the woodland path, I saw a large car park with an extensive restaurant and masses of people converging on the place in dozens of coaches. It felt strange and confusing to be suddenly back in civilisation and after a coffee in the restaurant, I escaped back to the woods.

The first serious rain of my journey so far began and it was on with my rain gear and a grim plod along a road, with cars splashing sheets of water at me. I gradually became aware of increasing numbers of cyclists passing me as I approached the town of Scherpenheuvel. A glance at the guide informed me that this was a really important pilgrimage centre, a Lourdes of Northern Europe. The tradition amongst Dutch, Belgian and German Catholics was to walk or cycle to this Marian shrine during the month of May. The old town, with its medieval concentric street pattern, is dominated by the Basilica of Our Lady, a beautiful baroque church.

A miracle: I was suddenly walking uphill. A glance at the guide and there was no doubt about it. The map now had contours and looming out of the misty sky were little low knolls, hillocks and curving ridges. The flat horizon was no more. It was my first real change of landscape since I had left the North Sea twelve days before. I was now 60m high – a vast altitude compared to the minus figures behind the dykes of the Lowlands. Despite the rain, my spirits were lifted.

I was booked into the Modern hotel in Kaggervinne and began asking people if they knew where it was. At a filling station a motorist knew its location and, as I suspected, it was off my route just outside the town of Diest. He offered to drive me there, which offer I gratefully accepted since I was now soaked.

A warm hotel room was welcome, as was a dry change of clothes. I had my spare clothes packed into waterproof bags inside my rucksack. As well as protection from the rain the packing of different items into separate bags made packing and unpacking really simple and I was usually ready to go within minutes each morning. My life as a nomad was already settling into an orderly rhythm and with all my possessions in one small pack, the sense of freedom was palpable. My daily need for quick access to small items such as money, wallet, guidebook, insect repellent and maps, was solved by a skier's type 'bum bag' strapped to my waist. Most days, however, I seemed to walk with a guidebook in my hand since in so many places the route markings were suspect, missing or few and far between. I began to manage John Hillaby's trick of reading while striding along.

A good meal ended one of my best days yet, although the distance covered was only 19km. Who cares? I had all summer.

22 May

The morning was dull and cool with heavy clouds promising more rain. I had a very late start and decided to return religiously to pick up the route where I had left off. This was a bad decision since it involved a long detour around the outskirts of Diest and up and down a green hill when there was a direct road right into the town centre. I wanted to visit this old town anyway since I had heard that it was one of the best-preserved medieval urban centres in Europe.

I passed through the intact ramparts and came into the town centre at the Grote Markt, where the Gothic church of Saint Sulpice dominates the square. Diest belonged to the House of Orange-Nassau, founded by William of Orange, known as William the Silent in the sixteenth century. This was an earlier William than the victor at the battle of the Boyne – the hero of the Protestant Orangemen of Northern Ireland. This earlier William's son, Philip-William, is buried in the Saint Sulpice church. Sitting in the square outside the church, I wondered if the Orange Order knew that the ancestors of their King Billy came from this most Roman Catholic of places.

The square was surrounded by seductive, tall brick houses of the sixteenth and seventeenth centuries. Their intricacies inspired me to attempt a drawing. Some of the elaborate gables

Grote Markt, Diest

had spiral volutes, oversized, at least in comparison to the typical Dutch gables in Amsterdam or Utrecht.

I left the town at midday through an elaborate town gate. The GR5 was well signposted on a wooden pole pointing south and marked North Sea-Riviera. I was always heartened when I encountered one of these impressive markers. They seemed to indicate and give me hope that not alone was the long journey feasible but that the route was well travelled.

I nearly posted a card in somebody's mail box outside their house. They were using an antique post box as their mail box. The Belgians love the kitchiest designs for post boxes. A little tiled roof, wendy house on top of a sawn-off log with stumps of branches – all made of concrete. I thought that Walt Disney would jump out of it.

The day improved and the dark clouds vanished. The Flanders province of Brabant was now behind and I was now entering Limburg. Another subtle change in the landscape slowly unfolded. The tracks were sandy; there were pines and stands of yellow broom. It was typical heath country. This region of Limburg is known as the Campine or Kempen. Hillaby walked down from the north through this area and found it infested with military training grounds, but here it seemed peaceful enough. I went wrong once, infuriatingly, since I did not see the red and white paint splashes which were partly hidden by fresh greenery. The route came smack up against a major motorway, the A2, howling with traffic but audible only when quite close and beyond the tree cover. The trail went parallel to the road but well below it for about half a kilometre and then turned away onto a heath. I was suddenly meeting walkers and in minutes hundreds of them, all going in the same direction as me. The fast ones sped past me without a greeting or a glance, but I gradually overhauled a small mixed group more or less ambling and these were intensely curious about my journey. They were amazed and, I think, a bit disbelieving that I was going to Nice. They were part of a once-monthly long-day walking group based in the town of Lummen which we were now approaching. They walked with me chatting for about an hour until our paths diverged on the outskirts of Lummen.

My hotel was still some distance away, at a big intersection of the A2 and another motorway, the E313. I passed under this motorway by a gloomy pedestrian tunnel and emerged to find a complex of modern buildings beside the ramps to the intersection. Directed to the hotel, designated a 'motel', I discovered it sandwiched between a large glass-fronted restaurant and various shops. The design was pure Western boulevard strip. It was called the Jardin Tropicana and the style was Mexican adobe vernacular with exposed plumbing, hacked-off partition tops, but with luxurious bathrooms, television and a mini-bar.

23 May

The Jardin Tropicana lived up to its name. The breakfast buffet was a cornucopia of delight: juicy yellow and pink sliced melons and cantaloupes, heaps of oranges, bananas, jugs of iced juice, bowls of every variety of cereal, stacks of breads, enormous cheese boards, all artistically arranged as a tropical feast. The cold meats and inevitable hard-boiled eggs came as standard. This was food for a long day's walk and a very long walk it turned out to be – over 28km.

I strode out with a spring in my step. My feet were not sore for once and I was brimming with energy. It was a national holiday in Belgium so there was no traffic and few people about. I came out on to the Albert Canal again and this great waterway curved away to the east towards Maastricht. The canal was constructed in the 1930s and linked the river Maas to the North Sea at Antwerp. In the early days the waterway was intended to facilitate the coal industry in the Kempen. With the decline of mining, the region is now mainly a conserved landscape with nature repairing the damage of past decades, but the canal is as busy as ever with barge traffic.

I stood on the bridge and looked down the canal. The official route of the GR5 was marked as a long, undulating and seemingly pointless detour through more suburbia before rejoining the Albert Canal at the distant Brug Stokrooie. A clear pathway led directly down the canal bank to the bridge and this seemed the logical route. In fact, this appeared to be the original route of the GR and was so described in the Sierra guide. Many of these detours appeared to be designed for local walk enjoyment and were highly frustrating to the long distance walker wanting to head south. My hatred of suburbia made up my mind and I set off down the canal.

This was a heavenly walk, not least because the direction was now nearly south, instead of the stubborn and maddeningly easterly drift of recent days. The day was turning out to be fine, the waterway shining, the path was on soft grass, traffic noise had vanished and, except for a few cyclists, I was alone in the landscape. An inviting curve of the canal's edge hid from view the distant bridge, the Kanaalbrug Stokrooie, and then I met my first lone walker – going the opposite way. He appeared to be a soldier with a pack. He was wearing battle-dress and looked morose, passing with only a barely grunted '*Gut morgen*'. I speculated smugly that he was on punishment drill. At least I was punishing myself voluntarily.

I passed the bridge and kept a keen eye for the turn off into the woods. A couple of kilometres of straight and delightful path led through pines, oaks and maples while the sky turned a brilliant blue. This was a national nature reserve called De Platwijers with little ponds full of noisy bird life, coots, ducks and herons. I came out of the woods onto a main road and the little village of Kiewit where there was the perfect café for my first morning stop. By now after thirteen days' walking, I usually stopped for a short rest after the first three or four hours each day. A delicious coffee was served on a tiny silver tray with three kinds of lump sugar, cream, a sliver of cake and a chocolate biscuit.

The marked route now zigzagged like mad, apparently to stay in the woods but eventually emerged into the magnificent park and arboretum of Domein Bokrijk. This originally had been a medieval Cistercian foundation with an abbey which became a state nature reserve and park in 1938. At the end of the park I arrived suddenly at the Kasteel Bokrijk and what seemed like swarms of people. This was a tourist honeypot with cafés and a large museum. The Openluchtmuseum Bokrijk is one of those local and regional history collections dedicated to offering a picture of Flemish country life, buildings and everyday objects of the past. Country life, as depicted here, has well and truly vanished throughout Western Europe, and now must be recreated to satisfy our nostalgia.

I sat down at a shady table in a pleasant garden restaurant and savagely contemplated my tired feet and a new blister. Was it ever going to end?

Studying the map I thought about somewhere to stay. Back at the tourist office in Herentals, planning my nightly lodgings through Flanders, I had noticed that the large town of Genk was exactly halfway along a one-day stage, my next. This gave an inviting prospect of a long day's walk without a rucksack if I stayed two nights at Genk and went by public transport back and forth to my bed.

The map showed a railway line, about a kilometre ahead, running straight to Genk. I was barely at the stop when along came a train and I was soon into the town's ugly centre. My hotel was old-fashioned but my room, though dark, was comfortable. I just fell into bed and slept.

24 May

I again appeared to be the only guest. How do hoteliers in Belgium make a living? This morning I had the worst breakfast so far. The old man who served me had not one word of English or French. We had an interesting conversation: I spoke single words of Dutch while he nodded his head.

I got a bus back to Bokrijk and rejoined the GR. Setting out without the infernal rucksack was strange. I felt unbalanced and quite giddy, as if I was about to float off. I settled down to an 8km walk back to the southern outskirts of Genk through a glorious paradise of heathland, dotted with little ponds and lakes. De Maten, yet another nature reserve, presumably salvaged from a landscape which had been devastated by mining and old industries, now abandoned. The ground was sandy and studded with silver birches. Startling lemon yellow bursts of broom speckled the young green of the oak scrub, while the ponds had chrome-yellow water-lilies and stands of tall bulrushes. The singing of blackbirds, thrushes and, what I thought was a nightingale, was mixed with the discordant croaking of thousands of frogs.

The outskirts of Genk gave me a rude awakening: ugly

suburbia and a disastrous café stop. When I entered, I was confronted by an individual who just stared at me with what felt like hatred. It seemed as if he could not believe that anyone would come into his café at eleven in the morning and that my arrival was a monstrous imposition. He grudgingly gave me a cup of dreadful coffee. He watched me drink every drop, radiating hostility. I paid and fled.

A fruit shop sold me a bag of peaches and I retired back to the woods for a slobberingly juicy feast, sitting under a shady tree out of the hot noon sun and then wiping my hands on my bare legs, now turning brown.

On a little lonely road outside Genk there was a curious incident. I was walking in my often abstracted way, lost in thoughts, plans, fantasies. I suddenly spotted a leather purse lying in the middle of the road. There was nobody about and indeed I had not met anybody for ages. It was heavy and contained a large amount of Belgian coins, amounting to about £5. There was no name or papers of any kind – just coins. I decided to hand it in at the next police station and walked on only to stop and ponder. Where would I find a police station? My deep resentment of having to diverge from my alloted route and add to my daily quota of kilometres was growing as each day passed. I realised that I would have to explain the circumstances, maybe fill in forms. To hell with it: it was only loose change!

I put the purse back down in the centre of the road and walked on. On an impulse I turned and spotted a cyclist behind me in the distance. When I calculated that he would be at the purse, I gave a quick glance back. He had stopped and was looking at the purse and then on to me. I kept walking but a quick glance back saw him take the purse up and remount. I looked straight ahead and felt him come up behind. He slowed but then speeded up without speaking to me.

After the dull, featureless outskirts of Genk were passed, it was forest tracks on soft paths all the way to the end of the stage at the little village of Zutendaal. Definitely rolling countryside now, memories of the dead flat Lowlands were fading.

A bus brought me back to the centre of Genk and my hotel.

I felt despondent. My feet were giving me hell and the thought of a long walk tomorrow did not help. I would, however, reach Maastricht and the end of the second stage. I was to meet Nanno Huismann there and the prospect of company and two days holed up in his house lifted my spirits.

25 May

I was the only passenger on the bus back to Zutendaal in the early morning. The driver spoke English and was very chatty. Walking again, I entered the woodlands and another nature reserve. For a change, it was misty with a cold drizzle. The woods were decidedly wet and I welcomed this after the heat of recent days. It was a lovely, lonely if damp tramp through silent woods.

I was beginning to parcel out the walk into sections, which made the enterprise seem more realisable. Logic and sense pointed to taking it a day at a time and not thinking too far ahead, but my imagination would not let me do this. I was often restless at the end of the day and could not resist turning the pages of the guides, unfolding the maps, calculating the day's achievement, adding up the score of kilometres so far, subtracting from the total and generally activating my brain when I should have been drifting into relaxed oblivion. Dividing the whole journey into sections of about ten to fourteen days' duration, with each corresponding to rough geographical regions gave me more confidence that I would eventually succeed. I now largely forgot the long-term goal and vowed to celebrate the end of each section.

The route zigzagged through the woods in the most drunken fashion, sometimes veering down forest rides, up and down sand dunes, while the map clearly showed a road leading down one side of a triangle to rejoin the route. I religiously followed the signs around the two sides of the triangle, sometimes feeling smug that I was doing it right and yet again cursing myself for being so rigid.

Coming towards me along one broad forest ride with dripping trees were two men, both with small packs. They greeted me cheerily in the way that fellow walkers do and I gratefully stopped for a chat, being starved of such contact for almost two weeks. I described them in my diary that night as 'two older men' and realised that I often do that, even though they were obviously much younger than me. Am I denying my own advanced years or, to put it optimistically, do I just feel younger or, maybe, just self-satisfied?

They told me that they were doing a 14km walk and asked where I had come from. When I told them, they were dumb-founded and had never heard of the GR5, even though they were on it.

I came into the small town of Lanaken on the Albert Canal, almost on the border with Holland. A seat on a café terrace gave me the opportunity to rest my tired feet. The coffee, accompanied by delicious and typical Dutch pancakes with sugar and maple syrup, was a delight. The pleasure of continental cafés and people-watching is hard to beat, particularly if you have worked hard to deserve it.

I arrived suddenly onto the canal again and this time continued straight down south along the bank of the now very wide waterway until I crossed back into Holland. This should have been depressing because I had left that country way back in Bergen-op-Zoom. The Dutch province of Limburg hangs down like an udder from the southern end of Holland; it is a long narrow region, bordered closely by Belgium on the one side and Germany on the other. The medieval town of Maastricht sits at the very end of the province and its old centre, with concentric streets and fortifications is on the banks of the Maas.

I had arranged to meet Nanno in the town centre, in the square known as Onze Lieve Vrouwe Plein. I had been there before some years back and thought I could find it easily, even though I had only a large-scale map. The GR5 continued straight down the canal towards Liège, so I now had a long diversion. I sat down on a suburban seat to wait for a bus to the centre, but none came. Eventually I walked all the way into the town and through the narrow streets of stone houses to the little square beside the magnificent Romanesque cathedral.

I had barely sat down at an outside café table when I saw Nanno's car drive into the square. We had a great reunion and drank some wine to celebrate my arrival at the end of section two.

Nanno's house was in Heerlen, a modern town some miles to the east, near the German border and the city of Aachen. A fast motorway brought us there and soon I was wallowing in the luxury of a long hot bath. Back then to Maastricht for a good meal in one of the many excellent restaurants in that most civilised of ancient cities. It was great to meet an old friend again. Nuala and I had known Nanno for nearly twenty years.

After so many lonely days and meals eaten in solitary silence a shared meal with conversation was bliss.

I think Hazlitt would have approved, since the pleasures of solitary walking were undoubtedly made more piquant by boisterous dinners in his evening's inn.

26 May

A day of rest! Clothes were washed, phone calls made and I even tried to read a newspaper in Dutch. I talked to Nuala and we made plans to meet at the end of the important section at Lac Léman. This was still a long way off, though, and when I worked it out – 355km covered and over 2,000 still to go – realism sobered me.

Nanno's house was a haven of rest: lots of books, music and a peaceful outdoor patio for sitting and talking. He lived alone. He was a teacher in a second-level school with the difficult job of dealing with Dutch teenagers who would rather be anywhere but school. Over the years Nuala and I had joined Nanno on some memorable mountain and country walks, such as the Stubai Alps in Austria. On the GR34, along the armoured coast of Brittany, Nanno gave us a fright by having a terrifying attack of gallstones. He had an awful night of pain but the next day quickly recovered and continued the walk. He carried impossibly heavy rucksacks and even added a collection of weighty stones whose shapes appealed to him.

I was looking forward to his and Nuala's support for the first stage of the long and difficult crossing of the French Alps in early August – if I got that far! We discussed the next stage I was to tackle: the passage down the Ardennes. I planned to walk the stage in nine days to the borders with Luxembourg and a different landscape. Nanno decided to join me for one day and since he had not walked the lower part of the province, said he would do the second last leg with me, from the village of Viesalm to Burg-Reuland. We made a hotel booking in Viesalm and agreed to meet there.

After exploring the modern city of Heerlen, we went back to Maastricht to enjoy this marvellous old place with its small-scale and intricate lacework of stone-lined streets. The Romans called Maastricht *Trajectum ad Mosam* because it lay at the easiest crossing point of the river Maas, or Meuse as it becomes later. The city stood at a real crossroads as well as within a network of frontiers. The Belgians, like the Dutch, had been ruled and dominated since Roman times by, among a host of others, the Holy Roman Empire, the Spanish, the Hapsburgs and the French. A resultant language line of demarcation runs across the country from east to west, with Flemish being almost exclusively spoken north of the line. To the south, the part known as Wallonie, the language is French. This line began outside Maastricht and Nanno said that in places a different language was spoken on opposite sides of a road.

I was about to step across this line. I looked forward to it, because I would now be able to read the guidebooks and at least attempt a conversation in French.

One day of rest was enough, so I decided to strike out the next morning. I was impatient to get on and vowed to do the next section in one go with no day of rest.

HOLLAND

● Maastricht

● Visé

● Nessonvaux

Spa ●

Ninglinspo ●

● Hockai

● Malmédy

GERMANY

Vielsalm ●

● Burg-Reuland

BELGIUM

0   10   20 KMS

LUXEMBOURG

Map 4: Ardennes

CHAPTER 3

Deep in the Ardennes

27 May

Nanno drove me back to the Albert Canal to rediscover the red and white flashes. Crossing the bridge, I was back in Belgium. My way was now generally south and, except for the plains of Lorraine, I would march firmly in the direction of my Holy Grail – the Mediterranean.

I spared a thought for Patrick Leigh Fermor here. On his walk, an even more eccentric one than mine, he wrote that when he was halfway to Constantinople, he was tempted by the accessibility of the Mediterranean and nearly put his expedition in jeopardy by turning south. He said that all northerners looking out at their dismal winter skies long for the pleasures of the warm regions below the Alpine passes. I remembered a friend, when I was talking about my planned expedition, asking me why I would not start at the Mediterranean and walk north? I told him that I could not conceive of such a plan; the pull of the south was irresistible. Walking south would bring me day by day to sunnier places, bluer skies, more exotic landscapes, balmier smells. It was, perhaps, a powerful metaphor for something else: a rediscovery of youth? Walking north could offer only cloudier skies, shorter days, civilised landscapes, the flat lands after the mountains and, at the finish, approaching winter and the cold North Sea.

Most of the earlier part of the day's walk was on farm tracks and paths, incredibly muddy after the previous day's rain. The mud was fine, creamy and clogging. I began to regret my choice of shoes over boots to save my feet. The mud stuck to my shoes until I emerged into a field of tall wet grasses which wet my legs but cleaned off the sticky stuff.

This was completely different country, with huge machines working enormous sand pits, ravines of rock, little hills and lots of climbing.

At the border town of Kanne, the famous Peter's Path, or *Pieterspad,* joins the GR5. This route comes down from the north of Holland at Groningen and is a more popular long-distance walking trail for the Dutch than the GR5.

I suddenly came out below the fort of Eben-Emael and a vivid reminder of this fought-over narrow corner of Europe. The fortress, constructed in 1933, is a stark monument to the blind belief in the efficacy of great fortifications to resist invasion.

The fort was gigantic, with a protective cutting forming a sheer drop of 40m to the Albert Canal. It was armed with dozens of guns in turrets and housed a full battalion of troops in deep underground bunkers. The incentive to build this vast construction came from a fresh memory of the swift penetration of the First and Second German armies, over a half a million men, in the Schlieffen Plan to encircle Paris in August 1914. This was the start of one of the most horrible and hopeless wars in history. The dense cluster of forts around nearby Liège were quickly overwhelmed by this invasion. The latest military architectural folly was to suffer an even more ignominious fate in 1940.

In the pre-dawn darkness of 10 May, eleven large gliders, filled with German sappers, silently landed on and around Eben-Emael. In a well-rehearsed plan, the sappers blasted all the gun turrets and in fifteen minutes captured the entire complex. The operation was timed to begin five minutes before the Panzers of the Sixth Army were to smash into Belgium on their way to the coast.

The defeat was so absolute and so contemptuously swift that for years locals believed that it had been the result of a treacherous German plot. It was rumoured that a secret colony of Germans, before the war, had, under the guise of growing chicory in nearby caves, filled these instead with enormous quantities of explosives.

Now I had a fresh guidebook and, with it, a new shock! The route descriptions were minimal and the maps, basic diagrams, were almost useless for finding your way down an intricate network of paths. The only advantage was that the guidebook was in French and I could understand it, although I needed a little help from my dictionary for important trail instruction words such as *emprunte, franchir, débouche.* I only hoped that the *balisage,* the trail markings, were frequent and easy to spot.

It was a quiet walk, except for the occasional rumble of trucks in the distant sand pits. I saw nobody for hours. This was in an area which, on the large-scale maps, seemed to be one great blight of roads and almost continuous cities and towns. Along the way was an extraordinary folly, described in the guide as a *construction curieuse,* which was intended as a sort of apocalyptic vision of the geomorphology and geology of the region. It appeared as a Gaudi-like chateau with four towers embellished with sculptures representing Michaël as sphinx, a lion as Ariel, a bull as Israël and an eagle as Anazel. The creator of this bizarre edifice was one Robert Garcet, described as a self-taught historian and archaeologist. In the Great War he was also a conscientious objector and evenly hostile to all countries, including his own, engaging in violence and warfare.

I must have been walking very fast since I arrived at the town of Haccourt at 2 p.m. I realised that I had crossed the language line now and tried out my French when ordering a coffee at a roadside café. The schools of my generation gave more consideration to classical study than modern languages, which meant that I had never had French as a subject. Years of travel on the Continent, using a variety of phrase books in French, Italian, Spanish and German, added up to almost total ignorance of any tongue but English.

Before I undertook this expedition, I had spent more than nine months going to evening classes in French and my excellent teacher, Patricia Del Monte, originally from Provence, brought me to a level where I hoped I could manage.

I crossed the Albert Canal yet again, and a short walk brought me across the Meuse into the town of Visé. The tourist office was closed, as usual, but a helpful woman directed me down the riverbank to a newly built hotel which, although expensive, offered me a splendid room facing the broad waters of the Meuse.

The window of my bedroom went down to floor level and looked out over the wide and dark river. A sunlit high cliff on the other side inspired a drawing. Bare slabs and buttresses of yellow beige rock were crowned by trees, while ledges and fissures had trailing vegetation and bushes, making a satisfactory texture of soft and hard, high light and deep shadow. I was the only foreigner in the dining room that night and the young

Visé, Belgium

waiter was attentive, friendly and was bursting for conversation. It was my first attempt at a serious conversation in French and I was woefully aware of my ineptitude.

Here was the test.

I managed to guess that he was telling me how he would love to travel, Belgium was dull and he was sad that he was only a waiter. It was depressing, but since he delivered it all with broad smiles it can't have been too bad or maybe I misunderstood the whole thing.

I apologised for my poor French but he rushed to assure me that my French was very good which, considering that I could manage only an occasional *bon* and *oui* and lots of nodding, was the sincerest form of flattery. Nevertheless, it did my confidence no harm and I became less and less inhibited about rattling off in the language at every opportunity.

28 May

My hotel was on the wrong bank of the Meuse for the GR, so I would have to back-track due north again.

Nothing doing. I was getting quite cunning at avoiding unnecessary detours. A careful study of the map showed a bridge downriver about 3 or 4km at Hermalle sous Argenteau. A minor road appeared to lead easily to the village of St Remy, marked by a church spire. My plan was to head for the spire and scout around for the GR markers. The path by the river was peaceful and traffic free in an early morning mist. I crossed the bridge and over the noisy motorway which bypasses Liège. A little road zigzagged up a steep slope and the spire of St Remy came into view, but where was the GR? I was now paying the price for straying off the waymarked trail.

I studied the nearly useless guidebook with its incredibly confusing maps. A correction slip in my copy apologised for a mistake in one map where the trail, marked in red, had been printed upside down.

A Belgian couple saw me looking at the guide and then at the woods where the route was to descend by a forest path. They showed me a small path leading downhill and said that this was the way to the GR.

The Sierra guide authors say that one of the unwritten rules for long-distance walkers is to beware the advice of the 'perfidious local' as to where the marked trail was. So far, I had not had to rely much on local knowledge but now I totally agree with them. Local people very often did not have a clue about footpaths and frequently gave wrong directions. In the months to come, that unwritten rule was to prove to be a useful one to obey. In this case, however, the advice was right! When I set off warily down a narrow path, the first red and white paint marks soon appeared.

The trail descended steeply by a slippery track into beautiful beech woods splendid in early summer leaves. A level forest road then followed and crossed the main motorway around Liège by a narrow underpass.

In the 1880s this city was expected to be in the front line of a possible attack from the east. On the orders of King Leopold II, the great military engineer Henri Brialmont constructed twelve great forts in a circle around Liège. They were all on high ground and were designed to protect the city against invaders. The forts were mainly underground, with gun turrets in mounds at the top of each. When the Great War began, the forts were run down and poorly manned. No trenches had been dug to connect the strong points, which were up to 3 miles apart.

General von Emmich had been given the task of opening the way to Liège with his Army of the Meuse. No large siege artillery accompanied his troops because it was contemptuously believed that the Belgian army would drift away like 'dreaming sheep'. But instead of slipping through the undefended gaps in the ring of forts, the Germans made frontal assaults. The slaughter from the fortress guns was a foretaste of the awful mass butchery of the Somme and Verdun. After the first battle of Liège, the Belgian newspapers had headlines celebrating *Les forts tiennent toujours*. The arrival of the huge siege guns on 12 August ended the euphoria and all the forts were smashed to pieces. Liège soon fell and the invaders surged towards the west.

I was walking along this high ground where the carnage had taken place all those years ago. Now only a peaceful forest of beech and chestnut trees covered the scene of the slaughter.

The trail suddenly came slap up against a thickly woven barbed wire fence. A large menacing sign inside stated *privé*. The only option appeared to be to go along the edge of a field.

This was planted in maize and the new young shoots came up the edge of the fence. It was impossible to walk along there without damaging the plants and I envisaged an angry encounter if I ventured that way.

What to do?

Returning to the barrier I eyed the trail disappearing into the woods. I thought I spotted a red and white marker on a distant tree and resolved that it was better to have a confrontation on the marked trail than on a field of maize. Padding the top of the massed barbed-wire with my rucksack and rainproof, I slid over into the trees. The trail marks appeared regularly and I went on, if a little apprehensively, my trail stick at the ready for an attack from a slavering hound. None appeared and I arrived at another barbed-wire fence. The same operation and I was back in legitimate territory.

I met the first of the dreaded variants today. These were options to the main GR and were also waymarked with the red and white *balisage*. Great care had to be taken not to wander off on one of these.

The village of Saive was a good marker for the correct route and this picturesque place was described as in *La vallée de la Julienne*. On again, strongly, along farm tracks past little villages, each with a tiny church: Tignee, Evegnée and Micheroux with its pretty stone houses. The grass-grown remains of one of the great forts, Fort d'Evegnée, were a monument to those two days of heroic Belgian resistance to the German war machine of 1914.

The country now opened onto large fields and I was always on the look-out for markers on distant trees, fences or walls. My day's stage ended at the village of Nessonvaux, on the banks of the Vesdre. I should have had a sense of foreboding when the guidebook mentioned the alternative GR de la Vesdre. The hotel was on a street corner and for once right on the waymarked trail. I went into the bar to ask for a room and came into a space blue with cigarette smoke and filled with men who all appeared to be roaring at each other. There was no television with football on view, so the noise was just good-humoured banter, I suppose.

The hotel was not the worst I have ever stayed in, but a luxury inn it certainly was not. There was one bathroom for the whole hotel and it appeared to be also the family's since one of them used it for an hour while this guest needed to go badly. My bedroom was decorated with the worst Catholic Kitsch: an elaborately decorated crucifix in glass, a simpering Virgin, and numerous photographs of family religious festivals. In startling contrast, the bathroom had a reproduction of an erotic drawing by Egon Schiele – a naked woman, legs sprawling provocatively.

29 May

I was glad to get away from that squalid place. Another lovely morning and a walk which went through glorious woods of beech and oak, on winding woodland paths and few roads. The rolling countryside with wooded hills, ridges, small meadows filled with wild flowers and occasional deep ravines was a joy. The Sierra guide had cautioned that care was needed where the variant trail, the GR de la Vesdre, crosses the North Sea to the Riveria route in several places. This was perversely often referred to as the GRV! The Americans had gone badly wrong here for most of a day and I was determined not to do the same.

The GR5 was well marked, however, but I was still uneasy since the maps in the guidebook were so poor and my large-scale one was purely decorative, showing a lacework of GRs all over the place. At first, it was a bit like entering the unknown, having to stop at each waymark to check with the guidebook description. This was good for my French but somewhat slow since I frequently had to consult my tiny dictionary for the exact meaning of different words. Was there a significant difference between a *route asphaltée* and a *chemin goudronné? Lisière* was a beautiful word, meaning the edge of the forest.

The village of Banneux is another popular pilgrimage centre where in 1933 a twelve-year-old girl claimed to have seen eight apparitions of the Virgin Mary. When I arrived it was crowded with pilgrims and dozens of tourist coaches. I was a solitary walker in the huge restaurant where all the talk appeared to be in German.

It was a Sunday and I met dozens of walkers in the woods, but few were chatty or even friendly. The maps in the guide were really infuriating and I wrestled and puzzled over two GR5 routes going in different directions, as well as a GR573 crossing and recrossing my trail. I finally managed to emerge from the Bois de la Porallée and wander down to the bank of the Ninglinspo stream. There was a pleasant sunny café terrace here and I threw down my rucksack and asked for a beer. The hotels all appeared to be further down at Sedoz-Nonceveux and I enquired from the waiter about these. He said 'Why don't you stay here?' He offered to show me a room. It had a window with a spectacular view of the oak-covered slopes and I took it at once. The drawback was that there was no bathroom in the building; a WC and a washbasin were located in a cupboard on the stairs landing. The distinctly non-voluptuous sensation of washing while standing up at a basin was tempered by an excellent evening meal with good wine.

On my way to bed I saw hundreds of swifts swooping and banking through the evening sky.

30 May

I awoke to a clear blue sky and the valley echoing with bird song. My bill for the night was 1,035 Belgian francs, about £20, for bed, breakfast and a three-course dinner.

Immediately I left the lodging I was climbing steeply up a narrow wooded ridge: almost alpine, with rocky escarpments. An early stage of the route followed a swift-flowing mountain stream which would become a torrent in wet weather. There were cascades and deep pools along the way, one of them called Bain de Venus. The sun was hot and the pool looked deliciously tempting, not least because of its name. I stripped off and sank into its cool depths. I lazily fantasised that a naked Venus would come out of the deep woods to join me but the reality was a violently lycra-clad, sweating male runner panting past and shattering the vision.

The trail continued up, increasingly steepening, and when I arrived on to the crest of a ridge there was delectably cool walking until I came out onto a plateau. I missed one of the hamlets I was supposed to pass, Basse Desnie. While thinking I was still heading for it I cursed the guidebook writer who said it was only 2.5km from my last fixed point. When I finally reached a village, I realised that it was the next one, Winanplanche. I had been walking far faster than I thought, despite the severe climbing. I was finally getting fit. A long serpentine route in the forest followed, with warnings in the guide to trust the waymarking. Through a stunningly beautiful deciduous forest and along a stream to a *fond sauvage* the trail landed me smack into the little town of Spa.

The peace had earlier been smashed by fighter jets roaring over. Close to Spa 'civilisation' was announced again with the infernal noise of lawnmowers. I mused about which was worst: NATO planes or pervasive suburbia. Belgians are certainly garden-proud. Nature is tamed, ruthlessly pruned, shaven, fenced and guarded by the *chien mechant*.

I sat in the Place Royale drinking a beer and read something about the place. Spa, *la perle des Ardennes,* 'has seen better times'. The most celebrated centre for medicinal waters since the Romans, it has attracted royalty and aristocrats for centuries. The great mansions now have a rundown, faded look, with peeling paint and Eurotrash souvenir shops, heaped with T-shirts, mugs, cuddly toys, jokey cards and funny hats, are everywhere. Nevertheless the little town is still a pretty place, set in a sheltered bowl surrounded by bosky slopes.

I found a hotel, had a rest, then dinner, wrote up my journal and retired for an hour with the awful, wonderful, Forsytes. Soames is so gloomy and pessimistic and so correct, I felt like a true Bohemian.

I passed through fields of new-mown hay that day. What a marvellous, almost forgotten scent.

31 May

The day began with clear blue skies and warm sunshine. This was the first May I have ever had all to myself. Every other early summer from school to college, both as student and later academic, has been a time for study and exams, a time of angst and incubus. Now I had been long enough on the trail to cast aside those memories and to enjoy the indulgence of being a vagabond.

I went off like a train, zigzagging up a steep slope to emerge out over the little valley of Spa. Then followed a fast, lovely, woodland walk of about 8km into the village of Polleur. I passed under the high graceful viaduct of the A27 motorway; thankfully the traffic noise died away before I had gone a 100m. I had been very careful of the warnings to watch out for the other GR, the GR de la Vesdre or GRV, which crossed the route about here. I found the junction and noted my own route, followed it for a short distance and then made a big mistake. I had arrived at the river La Hoëgne with the beautiful stone bridge, built in the late eighteenth century, and crossed over to take a photograph. I saw the familiar red and white paint signs on poles leading into the village and followed them to an enticing café with a shady terrace. I sat down for a coffee and studied my guidebook.

There was a strong warning under the heading *Attention* that the trail was beng modified around here owing to the construction of the A27 autoroute. Since the autoroute looked well completed, I was uneasy about following my guidebook, an old edition, published eleven years earlier. Foolishly I assumed that this was why the route led so obviously into the village when the book showed the trail on the other side of the river. The other GR had well veered off by now. I finished my coffee and noted another red and white sign on a pole opposite and duly followed the trail out of the village. After I had followed the well-marked paths for a while, the landmarks and turnings did not quite match the descriptions in the guidebook. My instincts and the First Rule of Long Distance Walking should have forced me to turn back, but the comment about route changes for the road construction and the admonition the day before to 'trust the waymarking' prevailed and I pressed on.

I then adopted the attitude, common to those who are lost

but will not admit it. I started to try to make the map and guidebook fit the increasingly changed countryside. The route was obviously going directly east instead of south-east and I got more and more demoralised but equally, if not more, pig-headed about not turning back. Eventually, though, I had to accept that nothing matched the map and that I was well and truly lost. Three hours and at least 12km later I came out to a large pond which had a café on its banks. There was a group of walkers here and they had a large-scale map. With their assistance I worked out what had gone wrong. I had followed a totally new GR. The walkers told me it was the GR Ardennes and this was not marked on any map I had and was not mentioned in my guide. I was a long, long way off my route on an already long day.

I checked my large-scale map. I was already almost off the edge and decided to walk back on roads to rejoin the GR5. After 9km of horrible road-walking, trying to avoid being mowed down by fast cars and trucks since there was no footpath, I arrived at the point where my GR should have appeared. There were no signs anywhere. It is always difficult to pick up a marked trail if you stray far away from its trace. I was now only about 7km from the village of Hockai where I planned to stay the night, but after walking nearly 40km in the heat I was finished. I arrived at the village of Solwater but the café where I wanted to phone for a taxi was closed. Just then I saw a bus leaving for Spa so I ran after it. The driver saw me and stopped. I explained my problem and he cheerfully agreed to find me an open café along the way. He did just that and did not charge me a fare. I waved him goodbye and became a full-blown capitalist again. Ordering an iced beer and a taxi, I stretched out and relaxed on a luxurious shady terrace with a view.

The taxi arrived in twenty minutes and I was deposited at my hotel in Hockai.

I consoled myself with the thought that it was an easy walk back to rejoin the GR5 the next day. I was very, very tired.

1 June

I felt I needed a short walk to recover from the débâcle of the previous day, although I was anxious to make my rendezvous with Nanno in Vielsalm on the evening of 3 June. Another splendid morning with a deep blue sky. I went past meadows of tall grasses, masses of buttercups and clouds of white and yellow butterflies. This was really beautiful countryside. I found the GR easily at a little bridge and set off this time very carefully, reading the guidebook and stopping to check my dictionary.

I was now, according to the guidebook, heading for the highlight of the trip through the Ardennes: a traverse of the wilderness called the Hautes-Fagnes. This is a high plateau of the Ardennes consisting of mainly moorland and scattered forests. John Hillaby managed to get himself lost there when he plunged off into the woods in pursuit of a black woodpecker. I hoped that I would not follow his example and that the waymarks would be clear. Almost at once when I entered the first coniferous forest, I was confronted by a large area of felled trees and no waymarks. I found one paint mark on a fallen trunk, but where now? I blundered on to the end of the felled section and was lucky to spot a faint paint splash on a distant tree.

I came out onto the open moorland of the Hautes-Fagnes near midday and marvelled at the wide space of marsh and the deep silence of the place. This is the highest region of Belgium, up to a maximum of 690m. It is now a huge nature reserve and is reputed to contain the remains of Roman roads. I wondered if these had been built by Julius Caesar, conquerer and Governor of Gaul?

A dry grass bank was an inviting spot to flop down, drowse and sunbathe for an hour. After a northern winter I could never resist the sensual pleasure of the sun on my body. Who cares about the dangers of the holes in the ozone layer? Just about everything pleasurable is bad for you nowadays. Such were my thoughts that freewheeling day in the high marshes.

According to the guidebook's crude map, I had to make a sharp right turn followed after a kilometre or so by a sharp left and another right. I arrived at a junction and stared in despair at a plethora of painted marks. The GR56 and the dreaded GRV. Not a GR5 in sight. Surely I could not have gone wrong again? There were few landmarks but I had followed the directions religiously and this time the map matched the country. Could that clump of trees ahead be what the guide called *la Clairière des Six Hêtres* (six beech trees)? I could count only five. I took a chance and kept pressing on. On a track near a stream bank, I met a party of middle-aged men, dressed inappropriately for walking in this heat. They were led by a serious and uncommunicative type who was busy with maps. The tailender was sweating like mad and wearing a tie. He greeted me sheepishly as if he knew he was out of his environment. Reflecting about this later, I realised that this long distance walker, already tanned, in rapidly fading blue shorts and with hair still close-cropped, must have looked equally bizarre to them.

I finally ran out of trail-markers. I backtracked but there was still no sign. Looking at the sketch map, I assumed that the stream was the Tros Marets and if I followed it I would be at least in the right direction. Abandoning all caution, I plunged into the thickets along the bank and struggled up and down to

Ardennes woodland

find a way out. I eventually broke through to a spectacular high-level path which the guidebook called *un magnifique sentier en corniche.*

I stopped here to admire the rolling wooded hills and the green, open grass slopes leading down to the valley and the town of Malmedy. I was only a few miles from the German border and began to reflect on how the Ardennes had featured so prominently in two world wars.

In 1934 the French General Pétain had declared that the Ardennes was *impénétrable.* This seemed to be a view which had persisted since Roman times when the area was described as 'savage and inhospitable forests'. In what became known as the 'Battle of the Frontiers', the German armies swept through here in August 1914 on their way to the coast, only to be halted eventually in Flanders. Despite this experience, it was still believed that the Ardennes was a barrier to invasion from the east. The Maginot Line, the ultimate folly of military construction, stopped well short of the Ardennes. On 11 May 1940 Von Rundstedt's panzers poured over the plateau and all along a wide front to attempt to reach the North Sea and cut off the Allied armies.

Four years later the lessons of the Ardennes still had not been learned. Following the successful invasion of the mainland of Europe in June 1944, the Allies freed most of France and Belgium. As the terrible winter of 1944 set in, the Americans were stopped short of the Rhine while the British débâcle at Arnhem condemned the Dutch, and particularly the citizens of Amsterdam, to a winter of near starvation as the liberation of Holland was postponed.

Nobody expected the panzers to emerge out of the snow-covered forests of the Ardennes again but they did, led once more by Von Rundstedt and catching the Americans napping. The offensive, aimed to penetrate again to the Atlantic, petered out in what became known as the 'Battle of the Bulge'. A quarter of a million Germans and 700 tanks pushed back the unprepared Americans in a last-ditch attempt to get to the coast at Antwerp and divide the Allied armies.

Malmedy down below me was infamous for the atrocity carried out by the SS. Over 100 American prisoners were rounded up, driven into the forest and machine-gunned to death. The massacre had the opposite effect, in that it stiffened resistance.

June 1994 was the fiftieth anniversary of the successful invasion and every town in this part of Belgium and indeed later in Luxembourg and France commemorated the event.

Malmedy was destroyed by bombing in the war, when the American Air Force mistakenly believed that it was still being held by the Germans. After the war it was completely rebuilt. The first hotel I entered seemed empty but the proprietor, a sour-visaged individual, glanced at me and my rucksack and said that he had no vacancies. I gave him a look and tried another hotel which booked me in without any fuss. This was the only time on my trek I was refused a room, except when the hotel was obviously booked out, and then I received apologies and help in finding an alternative.

2 June

I had a pleasant room on the ground floor, but in the middle of the night my deep sleep was disturbed by a noise upstairs; it sounded like a radio taxi, erupting in bursts of loud German. I stuck it for twenty minutes and then came out into the hall and shouted in poor French and direct English. 'That bloody thing is keeping me awake.' A sleepy voice eventually answered, 'I stop.'

Next morning the staff gave me furtive looks.

For a change it dawned gloomy and wet and it rained most of the day, with heavy cloud and mist on the hills and in the valleys. I had a long walk ahead and, in fact, welcomed the wet and coolness after the burning heat. It had rained all day on only two walking days so far.

My pace was fast and strong, the speediest of the whole trip, and I completed the day's stage in well under the guidebook time. I was walking with confidence, picking up the signs, and beginning to develop an instinct for the correct route. Could I be getting really fit at last?

There was a rude awakening along a riverbank when I slipped on a muddy slope and fell heavily on my left shoulder. It hurt a lot and I had to sit for a while to recover.

The infamous GRA crossed my route at the town of Stavelot and I carefully followed the instructions to separate me from it. At the edge of the town, the heavens opened. I ran into a café where my dripping arrival amazed a crowd of locals drinking beer at ten in the morning. During a brief lull, I escaped, but down came the rain again. The celebrated *Amis de la Nature auberge*, Les Gattes, was on the route and I called in for shelter and sustenance. I got a warm welcome from Madame and Monsieur and warmed my soaking bum at the huge pot-bellied stove while waiting for hot coffee. When I told the couple where I had started my walk, I was delighted to be told that the Canadian couple, Charlotte and Sven, last heard of in the Hook of Holland, were just four days in front of me. I was catching up. This was a boost to my morale since I thought that I had been moving very slowly.

The rain stopped and I had a fast cool march of 8km into Vielsam, another of the places destroyed in the 'Battle of the Bulge' and then rebuilt largely to reproduce the original form and details of the old fabric of the town. The hotel was very welcoming and I luxuriated in a long hot bath and later waited with a drink in the dining room for Nanno, who arrived promptly at 8.30, after which we enjoyed a good dinner.

This area is the German-speaking part of Belgium, comprising the Cantons de l'Est, and was returned to Belgium after the Treaty of Versailles in 1919. This wasn't my first visit to the German-speaking cantons. I had been here many years before with my second son Colm for an international orienteering competition and my memory of it was wet, wet woods and three days of non-stop rain.

3 June

It was good to set out walking again with a trail companion. I realised now how lonely long distance solo walking can become and that, even in this thickly populated part of northern Europe, I could walk all day without speaking to a soul. On that high *corniche* over Malmedy, I had looked out over a rolling sea of rounded green-forested hills without a building or road in sight. A glance at a large map of Holland and Belgium will show a dense cluster of cities and towns all laced together with a nightmare of roads. Who would want to go there to walk? The reality is that I had walked for weeks through what seemed like a huge forest of deciduous woods. The roads were just thin strips for stepping over, and even the huge autoroutes were often only glimpsed and their traffic roar diminished in minutes as the woodland paths wound on.

I was also well on target for the completion of my

programme to walk for nine days to the Luxembourg border without a rest day. This was an encouraging contrast to my stop-start progress through the Lowlands. As I strode along, I reflected that this was the longest continuous walk I had ever done: 500km and 24 days in the open air. I was getting fitter and stronger and taking it a section at a time seemed to be working wonders for my morale.

It was actually quite cold that morning as well as dull and unfortunately for Nanno the day's stage turned out to be dull also if not in fact boring. The country was very different now: a fairly open plateau with grassy knolls, fringes of trees and a definitely agricultural air about the place. The smell of slurry replaced the scent of new-mown hay. From my point of view, the walk was fairly direct and I rejoiced that I was moving rapidly south. Towards the end of the day we saw the valley of the Our, the first big river flowing south from the high plateau of the Ardennes. The Our eventually joins the Sûre, which itself merges with the grander Moselle. The joined waters then flow into the Rhine and again veer north.

Instead of woodland paths turning and twisting, giving tantalising glimpses of distant country, the open plateau was more like some of the early stages in the Lowlands with long treks along minor roads. Conversation replaced silent meditation and lapses into fantasy and I think I enjoyed the day more than Nanno since he found the road walking unadventurous. Low-flying jet fighters screamed over several times, making us jump with fright since the black shapes pass over before the shattering howls arrive. It was, however, a great day for bird-watching, particularly for birds of prey. We thought we saw a kite, but without binoculars could not be sure. The prominent forked tail was a possible clue. We saw several buzzards; one was being mobbed by two black crows. It continued its slow lazy flight, seemingly ignoring its tormentors. Kestrels quartered the ground in front and soared overhead for a wider view.

The village names were all German now: Braunlauf, Schirm-Grufflange and Bracht. After passing a *calvaire,* a wayside cross – a feature which increasingly became a landmark for the walker – the path dropped down into the small town of Burg-Reuland. Our hotel was old-fashioned and comfortable, with a large bathroom and lots of hot water for long deep baths to ease our stiffening muscles. There is nothing quite like luxuriating in a hot bath after strenuous physical exercise. Maybe this is just a masochist's apologetic: there is no pleasure without pain. Just the same, I was feeling better physically than I had for many a year and was convinced that I would go all the way to Nice even if it killed me!

BELGIUM

Burg-Reuland

Dasbourg-Pont

GERMANY

Vianden

Diekirch

Beaufort

Echternach

LUXEMBOURG

Wasserbillig

Wormeldange-haut

Luxembourg-Ville

Dudelange

Mondorf-les-Bains

0   10   20 KMS

FRANCE

Map 5: Luxembourg

CHAPTER 4

Luxembourg: River Meanderings

4 June

Nanno caught an early bus to return to his car. It was another dull and cool morning, promising rain. Almost at once there was a problem. The GR56 joined the GR5 here and the routes should have separated at the tiny hamlet of Weveler. Just at the exit to the village, a sign for the GR5 to Ouren pointed right but when I followed the waymarks, the route had no relation-ship with the, thankfully last, map in my awful Wallonie guide. Worse still, it also had no relationship with the first of my new 1:50,000 maps of Luxembourg. I trailed slowly along the marked route with a renewed sense of dread of yet another GR. The new map was detailed, however, and after a while I could see that the route was leading me in the general direction of the valley of the Our. I soon reached the riverbank and saw that a busy road followed all the meanders into Ouren. The footpath went off uphill to a high ridge above the river valley and after two hours I arrived onto open ground and smack up against a sign on the edge of a cultivated field. It was marked 'Luxembourg'.

I had arrived at the frontier but left it immediately to descend through dense woods to the river and the village of Ouren. When I entered a café, the first people I saw were two walkers complete with large rucksacks. We introduced ourselves and, after 26 days, I met my first fellow long-distance walkers on the GR5.

John and Marie, a Dutch couple, were planning to do a section of the GR5 every year until they completed it 'when we are 60'. He was 48. This long trail taken in stages, I found out, was a fairly common enterprise amongst Dutch walkers.

I walked most of the day with John and Marie: welcome company after a long solitary spell. They told me about a Dutch woman who was walking alone all the way to Nice and who had just teamed up with two Scotsmen; they were one day ahead of us. Things were looking up. It was a huge boost to my morale to find that I was not the only lunatic on the trail, and the prospect of catching up with fellow walkers gave a sense of anticipation to each coming day.

Outside the village there was a large monument dedicated to a United Europe and at this point we crossed over the frontier into the Grand Duchy of Luxembourg.

There were, in fact, three frontiers here: Belgium, Germany and Luxembourg. The Grand Duchy is only about 80km long, but the GR5 through the country is over 200km, largely following the meanders of the Our, Sûre and Moselle. I planned to take nine days to get to the French frontier.

The motto of the Luxembourgers is *Mir woelle bleiwe wat mir sin,* we wish to remain what we are. Considering that they have been conquered, invaded and trampled on through the centuries by Burgundy, Germany, France, Spain and Austria it is a wonder that they are different at all. The language, Luxembourgeoise, is strange, largely a mixture of German and French – but it sounds at times more French than German in its intonation. French is the language used for most business. It is the third richest country in the world, after Switzerland and Lichtenstein, and looks it. With a population of only 390,000, there are more cars per head of population than anywhere in Europe. Money is, of course, the answer because Luxembourg is a large banking centre and tax haven. It is also a major location for European institutions, including the European Parliament.

I now had a fresh guidebook, one I had bought in Amsterdam. It was new and covered the stretch from Ouren to the start of the climb up to the Vosges. The wretched Wallonie one was now discarded. The new maps were also a relief, although the scale of 1:50,000 was still not detailed enough to cope with the intricacies likely to be met in this long-inhabited part of Europe.

We had a lovely, if very long, walk all day on forest paths, sometimes along the riverbank, at other times short-cutting a meander of the river with lots of steep up and down. I was very tired after nine days from Maastricht without a rest period and was glad to see the bridge at Dasbourg Pont appearing around a bend in the river. The café at the crossing had no rooms and I was directed over the bridge into Germany where there was a hotel on the opposite bank, in the village of Dasburg. The Dutch couple went on and we agreed to meet later, possibly at Vianden.

The hotel appeared to be full of walkers and motorcyclists but they found me a room. I found the dining room crowded with boisterous German youths. It seemed that they had been for a long and unaccustomed walk and were now celebrating in the best of humour with beer drinking and singing. When this was followed by a competition which consisted of pairs chasing up and down the dining room giving each other fireman's lifts, I retired to bed.

5 June

I was first down for breakfast but had to wait for 30 minutes until the staff got organised. A few of the young roisterers of the evening before crept silently and sheepishly into the dining room, their voices low.

I went back down the road to the bridge over the frontier and recalled Hillaby's antics with the border guards. He walked back and forth into the centre of the bridge from the Luxembourg side, stopping as the official on the German side came out of his hut each time to face him. Poking fun at German officialdom, he felt, may have been childish, but he enjoyed it. The custom hut was now deserted and I crossed yet another of Europe's vanished frontiers.

I was on my own again and though I missed the companionship of the previous day, I consoled myself with Hazlitt's eulogy on the virtues of solo walking. He wrote that, if you have companions:

> *You cannot read the book of nature, without being perpetually put to the trouble of translating it for the benefit of others. I am for the synthetical method on a journey, in preference to the analytical. I am content to lay in a stock of ideas then, and to examine and anatomise them afterwards . . . I like to have it all my own way; and this is impossible unless you are alone . . .*

The route led up through the wet woods and out on to a windy plateau. I lost the waymarks coming down the hill and landed back on the N10 which ran along the riverbank. The planners of the trail were obviously trying to keep away from this road and took the route up and along the high ground overlooking the river valley. Maddeningly, this meant constantly winding up and down the slopes, occasionally hitting the road for a few metres before going back up. I now encountered another perversity of the GR5 when it entered the Grand Duchy. They had changed the waymarks!

Not once but four times they were changed along the stretch of the trail through Luxembourg. I had been alerted to this in a small boxed notice in the new guide: *Contrairement à la signalisation internationale des GR, le tronçon du GR5 traversant le Luxembourg est balisé comme suit* . . . It went on to describe the different waymarks to look out for along the route of the GR5: from Ouren to Beaufort, a yellow round disc; from Beaufort to Ecternach, a green triangle on a white ground; from Ecternach to Wellenstein, a yellow rectangle and from Wellenstein to the French frontier, the yellow round disc again.

Did I detect a note of asperity in this notice? The new guidebook had after all been published by the French the Federation for the *Randonnée Pédestre*. It certainly was contrary to change the long-established red and white markers, recognised internationally and which had lovingly led me from the North Sea. If the Dutch and the Belgians could adopt the simple and easy-to-spot French system for long distance trail marking, it was understandable that the originators of the system would be exasperated by the pig-headedness of the Luxembourgers. Maybe this had something to do with their desire to remain the same as they always were – different.

I cursed and swore about this system for the nine days through the Grand Duchy. Not alone did my beloved red and white marks disappear but there was no continuity to the GR5 along the way. The yellow discs, the green triangle and the yellow rectangle were all markers for different internal paths through Luxembourg and just shared the (now totally unrecognised) GR5, for certain stretches.

No wonder Luxembourg is one of the richest countries in the world: the walking tourists get trapped and walk around in circles within the borders of this benighted place – spending all their money!

I found myself talking out loud like this as I extricated myself from a thicket of nettles to try to find the right path. On one section I could locate no yellow discs at all, so I continued down to the road and along the river. It was peaceful on this Sunday morning, little traffic and lots of bird song, late cuckoos as well as the usual melodious blackbirds, and the sound of the fast-flowing water as I marched along.

The morning started cold with heavy showers. When I made one foray up into the woods, the sun came out just when I arrived at the top of a high bluff overlooking the river. I sunbathed here for twenty minutes, enjoying a stupendous view down into the green wooded valley. The newly waymarked international long distance route, the E3, joined the GR5 along the way. This route goes from the Atlantic coast of France eastwards to the Danube and then on to Istanbul. The new name for the GR5 is E2 and the maps now showed the two sharing the same trail all the way to the end of Luxembourg. I never referred to my route as the E2 and did not meet anyone else who called it anything but the GR5 or *GR Cinq*. E2 and E3 sound like motorways and I hope the designations do not stick.

I mused about the names of long-distance routes. There was a definite attraction to geographical names: the Appalachian Trail; the Pennine Way; the Kerry Way, and historic routes like the winter Art O'Neill walk. This Irish Chieftain of Tudor times escaped from Dublin Castle across the snow-covered Wicklow mountains. The French have the Tour Mont Blanc and the marvellous circular traverse of the Dauphine, called the Tour d'Oisons. Some of the numbered GRs have become famous: the GR10 traverses the Pyrenees; the GR20 comes up the centre of Corsica, while the GR34 follows the coasts of Normandy and Brittany.

I came into the old town of Vianden in the late afternoon and met John and Marie at the bridge.

I decided that this looked like a perfect place to rest for a day. Ten days' walking without a break was enough.

6 June

The town of Vianden is dominated by the 1,000-year-old château perched on top of a wooded hill. The castle was the seat of the House of Nassau, ancestors of the Dutch Royal family. The restoration of the structure was still in progress and the story of the reconstruction was part of the display inside. On the night I arrived, the floodlighting made it a magnificent spectacle. Victor Hugo is also celebrated because he chose Vianden for his self-imposed exile in 1871. His house is now a museum. The town is splendidly situated on both sides of the Our as a tiny enclave of Luxembourg pushes back the German border from the riverbank.

I booked into a hotel right on the bridge for two nights and in the morning strolled up the steep hill to look at the castle. An ideal opportunity for a drawing since I had not stopped for one since Visé. I found a private place to try to make something from the jumble of Romanesque fortifications and Gothic pinnacles rising out of the lush leafy hill. Nobody bothered me. I hate to have someone standing behind me watching me sketch.

Vianden, Luxembourg

I had a leisurely lunch with a glass of Moselle and reflected that I would soon be entering wine country for the first time, proof that I was entering the southern regions. It was another cool, almost cold, day with people grousing about the weather, just as they do in Ireland. More like the winter, they said.

This was the fiftieth anniversary of the invasion of the European mainland, 6 June 1944, and the shops had books and pictures of that time on display. A short distance north of the town there is a monument commemorating the 1st American Armoured Division, led by General Patton, the first Allied troops to enter Germany from Luxembourg.

It rained that night and mist closed in all over the valley.

The château on the hill was almost invisible. I had arranged to meet John and Marie for a drink, but they never turned up. I heard weeks later that John's father had become ill and they had had to return home.

7 June

My destination was Diekirch, a short walk of 18km. The pains in my legs had returned, as well as the shoulder trouble and I was having difficulty lifting my rucksack each day. A short day, I hoped, would improve things. As it turned out, I was often just as weary after a short day as a long one. If I did a really long stage, I was exhilarated, while a short day sometimes left me gloomy. Focusing on distance to be covered and targets to be met meant that I wanted to keep moving at a regular pace. This was why rest days never satisfied me. I felt caged. The targets were slipping behind and not allowing me to settle into a nice restful torpor. I usually went for a walk on my rest day.

The morning sky was blue with little puffy clouds. I felt stale and stiff but as the day turned warmer began to feel better. The truth is that although I felt that I performed well when the days were cool and even cold, I found the dull wet weather for the previous five days was really depressing. The sun was now well up and it lifted my spirits. The birds were singing, the larks soaring and the walk was lovely. There were quiet rural roads to start and then a magnificent march through a forest of tall beeches along the crest of a hill. When I came out of the forest, there was an immense panorama of low, rounded hills covered in dense woods. Not a road, not a town, not a house to be seen. No noise of traffic. This was the Our valley with a rolling ocean of green on the Luxembourg side and beyond the German bank the forests stretched into infinity.

I reflected again that this was, on the map of Europe at least, the most urbanised, the most road-desecrated and the most densely populated region of Europe. I had seen nobody all day and the landscape looked as it might have done before Caesar's legions marched up from Rome. My diary that night recorded how I had felt that day.

> *Look at a map of Holland, Belgium, Luxembourg, northern France and west Germany and you will see a vast concentration of big cities, a network of roads with the motorways a thick complexity of red lines and you will feel that there could be no countryside left. The reverse is the truth. I have walked now for a month through this concentration of transportation routes and urban spread and have never, except for my short foray into Maastricht (and it is small) been in any large inhabited place. I have briefly seen, passed under or over, major motorways but in all cases in fifteen minutes on either side the sight and sounds were gone. Take heart – there is plenty of green space left and this is the way to prove it. Walk the country.*

The day ended on a path by fields of green shimmering barley, dotted with outrageously scarlet poppies. I diverted from the trail into the small town of Diekirch but after a beer on a terrace, decided I didn't like the place. The sprawling campsite on the riverbank made up my mind. I walked back to the route where I had spotted a modest hotel beside the old bridge.

This was the end of the first of three short walks I had planned to help me recover my energy and cure the pain in my legs and shoulder. I hoped it would work.

8 June

When I paid my bill, I found that I had a room with bathroom, breakfast, a good dinner and several glasses of wine all for about £20. I wondered if things are getting cheaper as I move more into tourist country and there is more competition? It was a magical walk that morning through a beech forest, dark after entering it from the bright sunshine, with the heavy green canopy of early summer. The bird song was deafening. In one clearing, shot with shafts of light, I had to stop to listen to an extraordinary recital from a solitary blackbird.

There is a real message of hope when you walk like this through miles of green countryside, by meadows of wild flowers, fields of barley and immense areas of deciduous woods. Maybe Greenpeace is right to cry wolf, for he may eventually come, but there is absolutely no doubt that Europe is still beautiful and green, much as it has been for thousands of years. The morning had started in thick mist, a woolly blanket which promised to lift, and shortly did, into a day of hot sun. By the mid-afternoon the heat was oppressive and I was drenched in sweat, with the damned rucksack making an increasing damp patch in the small of my back. I discovered that I had lost my water bottle, so I bought a large plastic bottle in a supermarket to keep me going. This added to the weight on my back. After a while I felt that I was sweating more than usual but when the moisture ran down the backs of my legs, I stopped to discover that the bottle had split and that the inside of my rucksack was full of water. I had to remove everything and try to dry off each separate item as best I could. Nothing to drink now and several hours before the next village.

At one point the track ended in a confusion of fallen trees, obviously storm damage. After several forays left and right to find the trail again, I had to walk slowly around in ever-increasing circles until I spotted a red and white mark in the trees. I did a compass check to make sure that I was not going back the way I had come.

A winding woodland path, snaking between clustered pinnacles of bare rock, led me into an area known as 'Little Switzerland' because of the extraordinary formations of sandstone outcrops. When I emerged from the woods, I saw the old village of Beaufort, perched above the river gorge. Thirst drove me into the first hotel. Several cold beers were heaven and I drifted into a delicious lethargy. The thought of picking up the pack again was unpalatable and when the barman appeared I asked the price of a room. He quoted me 1,700 francs, demi-pension, for a room for one. Paradoxically, it was less if two were sharing. I said that this was too much. He went off and returned to offer me bed, dinner and breakfast for 1,400. I gratefully accepted and was shown up to a cool, quiet room in this Auberge Rustique. This was my first experience, and a lesson, in bargaining for a night's lodging.

After a shower and a long rest, I went out to explore. Beaufort was notable for its two historic buildings, one a medieval castle founded in 1100, and a Renaissance château of 1649. It was a cooler evening and I enjoyed drawing the ruined castle. At dinner that night the guests were all Dutch and none of the parties seemed to be interested in conversation with the solitary diner. In a mood of self-pity, I went to bed early and read my regulation ten pages of the Forsytes.

9 June

I had now completed about one-quarter of my walk to the Mediterranean, 636km. My first thought was that this was great news, but then I did a swift calculation. Allowing for my planned break after Lac Léman, and multiplying by four meant that I would not cross the Maritime Alps until the end of September. I was told that the first snows of winter can fall in the southern Alps from the middle of that month.

I would have to speed up. Thirty days and 636km was only 21 per day. I gloomily recalled John Hillaby's terrifyingly long daily marches, sometimes continued through the night. How would I do it? Fewer rest days and longer stages were the only answer, and I marched off that morning full of determination to do better.

I immediately entered an extraordinary forest. The walk all day was through the *Petite Suisse Luxembourgeoise,* a dark green world with paths winding up and down steep staircases of rock and in and out of narrow ravines, some only one metre wide, squeezed between grotesque sculptured cliffs. Rivulets and streams were everywhere and the bizarre rock scenery was obviously the result of intense erosion of the soft sandstone.

Several of the outcrops had strings of rock climbers and I stopped to watch the struggles of roped individuals desperately trying to follow the instructions of leaders firmly belayed above. It was evidently a school of climbing. This had been my favourite, obsessive, sport for nearly twenty years. I had joined the first mountaineering club in Ireland in the late 1940s while in my second year of college. Rock climbing quickly became a passion and weekends were eagerly awaited for the exploration of new routes on freshly discovered crags. In the 1950s Snowdonia in North Wales tempted us to try the classic climbs on the fantastically named Dinas Y Cromlech, Clogwyn Y Grochan and Clogwyn du'r Arddu.

A serious Alpine accident in 1967 had ended my career as a rock climber. Watching the frantic moves of one young person on a glorious rock wall, riddled with what climbers call 'jug handles', made my fingers itch to try it again. My memories of climbs ranged from the pure terror of 'no going back' moves to the sheer sensual delight of flowing up a delicate slab, and the triumph of overcoming a hard final pitch with dramatic 'exposure' below. Those days were gone; there were new pleasures in exploring the countryside and mountains, but I missed the drama of steep rockfaces.

It was cool under the thick canopy of tree tops and I now met numerous walkers, this being a major centre for day excursions. The perverse trail markings were further confused by the side paths to various promenades; *Kippiglay, Gorge des Brigands, Sieweschloeff* and the wonderfully named *Zigzagschloeff,* Zigzag Gorge. There is also a Wolf Gorge, *Wolfschlucht* and a Cleopatra's Needle. All the people I met spoke Dutch, German or Luxembourgoise and, as walkers usually do, greeted me cheerfully.

I came out of the forest abruptly to see the pretty little town of Echternach on the Luxembourg bank of the river, now the Sûre. The town was dominated by the magnificent Benedictine Abbey, founded by Saint Willibrord from Northumberland. Echternach was obliterated in 1944 in the Battle of the Bulge where the front line stretched north to Malmedy. Everywhere there were memorials, mainly to American troops killed in that winter battle. The astonishing thing is that this 2,000-year-old town was entirely rebuilt, using traditional materials, to replicate exactly what had been there before that terrible winter of 1944/45. The Romanesque basilica with its high stone bell tower, the Gothic Town Hall, the Roman villa, as well as the fabric of the ancient market square, streets and façades, were replaced, amazingly, in only three years.

It looked as if I had just missed the great annual event in Echternach – the homage to Saint Willibrord which is held on Whit Tuesday. The festival is known as the *sprangprozession*, a dance procession. The story is that in medieval times a man who had been condemned to death was asked to state his last wish while standing on the scaffold. He asked for his violin and immediately played a fast hypnotic tune which had everyone dancing so madly that they could not stop. In the confusion the convicted man vanished. In the festival nowadays the crowds dance along behind marching bands for hours. Since 1975 this has become one of the great European festivals of music and dance.

I found a friendly hotel and went out to explore, eventually attempting a drawing of the impressive basilica.

I had covered only 16km that day. So much for my determination the night before to do better.

10 June

It was a dull cool morning, the weather forecast was bad but I resolved to do a long stretch, with the French border now firmly within my sights. I covered the first 12km very fast, in well under three hours, and had no trouble with the markings. This was in spite of being greeted by my guidebook with a warning to watch out for a change in the waymarks to a yellow rectangle. The second half of the stage was to be different, however. As I came out of the tiny village of Girsterklaus, it started to rain heavily. I was walking in shorts and, even though the water ran down my legs and filled my shoes until the leather was soft and soggy, it was still better than clammy trousers – or so I rationalised. A waymark appeared which, like many in Luxembourg, was mounted on a neat, metal post. It looked suspicious, as if it had been twisted around. I had come across several places where signs mounted on poles had been turned away from the correct direction. Was some joker at it again?

There were several tracks ahead and I tried each, but all ended in overgrown paths. The track indicated on the sign was my last choice. It divided and divided again without any further waymarking. It was a maze with no way out. Cursing the Luxembourgoise eccentricity, I gave up and, trusting the lie of the land, plunged downhill to reach the road, which I knew ran along the riverbank. I fought my way through nettles and brambles and over an abandoned dump until I heard traffic and broke out onto the road.

A check of the map showed that I was further back than the place with the dodgy signpost on the higher level. This was on an already long day and the prospect of walking a road with fast traffic and no footpath did not improve my temper. After 2km of suffering I could see a way uphill again to rejoin the path along the top of the escarpment. The first yellow rectangle appeared and I dutifully followed others which led me up a steep slippery track to the top of a hill and then promptly back down again, this time on slippery stone steps. It was just a viewpoint. I tried again but could find no way out of the confounded place. In a bad mood and very damply, I went back to the road and grimly plodded along towards my night's destination, the town of Wasserbillig.

Crossing under the giant viaduct carrying the A48 autoroute, I came out into open country and saw my first vines. Into the warm south at last! As if to celebrate this event, the rain stopped, the sun came out and I could stand and wallow in this novel view of sweeping slopes and vine terraces stretching out on both sides of the river. Sylvaner is the wine most available hereabouts and I had been offered it for most of my time in Luxembourg.

The Moselle, a larger flow, joins the Sûre at Wasserbillig and the (now wide) waterway continues as the Moselle. I found a hotel at a road junction in the centre of the town. It proved to be a mistake in more ways than one. The night-time traffic over the bridge into Germany was non-stop and noisy and the building was a ramshackle place, dirty and smelly. There seemed to be no alternative so I decided to put up with it. A few glasses of the local *vin blanc*, Rivaner, helped to relax me after a satisfactory 25km covered that day. The dining room was full of elderly folk, eating the same meal, and obviously involved in the exercise I had seen earlier in Belgium, a day out being subjected to the soft selling of household items nobody really wanted.

11 June

I decided to give myself an easy day. My feet really needed it and my knees had hurt in bed during the night while I was kept awake by traffic noise. I couldn't get away fast enough from this wretched excuse for a hotel and took a short cut up the riverbank to rejoin the GR at the town of Grevenmacher. A plaque here commemorates the passage of Napoleon in 1804 through the *departement des Forêts*, now the Grand Duchy of Luxembourg. The route led up steep stone steps, appropriately a Station of the Cross, to an architectural gem of a simple pure white chapel. The map showed the trail going out along the edge of the escarpment above the river, but new construction had removed all signs of the route and indeed the track itself. I found a little lane which wandered back to the waymarks in a short distance. There were wonderful views now down to the Moselle and across the other side to the rolling vine terraces of Germany.

The Moselle

The clattering bellow of a helicopter filled the air and, to my consternation, I saw the ugly machine flying low, obviously spraying the vines over the ridge where I was heading. I could smell the chemicals and tried to cover my face with a small scarf I had for colder weather. When I came out on the top, I found myself beside the thing, now on the ground where there was a refuelling station. It looked like a sinister death machine, with wide metal arms for spreading the poisonous mist. I hurried on to escape the next deadly flight and where the vines ended at a small village, I came on a sign with a skull and crossbones and a warning that a helicopter was spraying.

Where had I read about the eco-friendly wines of Luxembourg? The guidebook quoted a eulogy on the wines of the Moselle, the white wines of 'superb quality': Riesling, Silvaner, Rivaner, Elbling, Auxerrois, Pinot blanc, Pinot gris and Gewürtztraminer. How does this claim fit in with what I had just experienced? If the chemical spraying needed a warning sign, then surely the wine bottles warranted it also? I still continued to drink the stuff but with a degree of cynicism.

At a panoramic viewpoint above the village of Wormeldange a small hotel on the high point attracted me with its advertisement for a *belle-vue terrasse*. It was early afternoon but I felt I needed to indulge myself. The friendly proprietress showed me into a huge, luxurious bedroom with a balcony overlooking the river. What a contrast after last night's dump. After a long shower I washed my clothes, wrote letters and cards home but mostly sat on the balcony, enjoying doing nothing. I was by now really slipping into the simple life of the wanderer. All my possessions were in one small bag. Packing and unpacking took two minutes. There was no car to park and nobody else to wait for or fit in with. I could be gone in a few minutes and disappear into the woods, leaving everything behind me. This was the life.

12 June

Church bells woke me – it was Sunday – and from my balcony I saw a clear blue sky and early sunshine shimmering on the waters of the Moselle. The breakfast was superb. I had discreetly bundled up a few rolls with ham and cheese for my lunch and where this was possible it was my best way to ensure a snack on the trail. I used also to stock up on chocolate bars to last a few days. Occasionally I went hungry, but the problem of thirst was far greater as each day got hotter. After the bursting of my large plastic bottle, I settled for several small bottles and topped these up where I guessed the tap water was drinkable. I took chances, but since some sources were actually labelled *potable* or *non-potable,* I got away with it.

I met nobody all day. It had been three days since I had met another person on the route and my thought was that my next encounters would be in the more popular Vosges Mountains in July, unless I caught up with some walkers ahead. This was always an attractive prospect to savour and it lessened the loneliness of the long distance trail. The sun was getting hotter and hotter but on the ridge there was a brisk cool breeze which kept me bounding along. There was a musical clamour of church bells coming up from villages all along the river and larks sang incessantly high above. I came on the dreaded helicopter again, looking like an evil giant insect with its outstretched tentacles. They were tinkering with it, fortunately, and muttering maledictions at it. I hurried on, anxious to get out of range of the clouds of chemical mist which would go everywhere in the strong breeze.

Although the trail was mainly along the ridge above the river and by one of the many *chemin viticole,* it made frequent forays down to little villages on the banks of the Moselle, now getting wider. At one of these, Ehnen, there was an unusual circular church, dating from 1826, as well as a wine museum. At the tiny hamlet of Stadtbredimus I had a delicious filter coffee at a terrace café, sitting in the sun and reflected for the nth time that this wasn't a bad life after all. Hazlitt would have approved.

We go on a journey chiefly to be free of all impediments and of all inconveniences; to leave ourselves behind, much more to get rid of others.

Up into lovely cool woods where there was a *parcours,* an exercise park, laid out. This idea came from the USA when it dawned on Americans that eating giant doughnuts, hamburgers, frankfurters, crisps, buckets of popcorn and consuming gallons of Coke could make you fat. In the 1970s I first saw one of these parks laid out along the waterfront in San Francisco. Dozens of earnest and sweaty men and a handful of women were pulling themselves up on horizontal rails, bending and stretching at different stations. It looked like torture. The *parcours* was empty, even though it was Sunday. Maybe Europeans are lazier or more sensible about what they eat. I took a self-portrait, balanced on a log.

Down to the pretty town of Remich where the waterfront was busy with boats, water scooters and promenaders. The place was a blaze of flowers in gardens, window boxes and baskets. Up again, steeply, to the ridge where there was a viewpoint. I stopped to rest and have my lunch sitting at a picnic table while I studied the map. The route, perversely, went off up the road for Mondorf-les-Bain, my destination for that evening, but after a kilometre it zigzagged down to the river, only to come right back up again. By continuing along the road, which was relatively free of traffic, I could go straight to the town in half the distance. I kept going along the road. The E3 left the GR5 here and went off south and east to Istanbul.

I came into Mondorf-les-Bain and the French frontier – a significant milestone. The place seemed to be full of hotels, many ornately embellished and a few delightfully Art Nouveau. In the first half of the century this was a fashionable thermal resort and, although now passed its peak of popularity, was still functioning as such. Most of the hotels were expensive for a single person and a one-night stay was not welcomed. I settled for a little place on a side street which was run by a Chinese family: basic but cheap. Leaning out of my window, I heard a brass band coming along the street. The marchers ranged from old men to little boys and girls, dressed in dark blue uniforms. They made a great sight swinging along, drums thumping, to play in the park.

A Chinese meal that night made a change from the increasingly repetitious Luxembourg menus. I drank more of the Rivaner, which I found out was a blend of the Silvaner and Riesling grapes – a pleasant dry and fruity white. There are Roman sites all along the Moselle in Luxembourg and the viticulture dates from those days.

13 June

I entered France but after fifteen minutes came straight back out again. The depressing thing about the next stage was that for a day and a half I had to walk back due west. The route followed all along the southern border of Luxembourg before turning due south again to enter Lorraine. I imagine that this has something to do with avoiding dull country because the maps show more woodlands to the west. It does, however, swing away from the Moselle, only to rejoin the river further south near the old city of Metz. It would seem logical to continue down the river but I figured that rights of way may have been difficult to find. Just the same, it was so frustrating for me, in my zeal to go south, to have to march off in a different direction.

Immediately after I left the hotel the waymark pointed across a little footbridge which had a sign, *France,* and a stern warning not to cross. The paint was fading on the lettering, and rank grass and weeds grew around the deserted border post. Despite the warning, I triumphantly entered France. Nobody cared, however, in this new borderless Europe. The route followed a little stream for about a kilometre and then came back into Luxembourg.

I was now on a high rolling plateau with open country visible for miles. Great fields of emerald green barley were waving in the breeze and there were sudden exotic patches of scarlet poppies. Away in the distance, however, was a reminder of industrial Europe: huge cooling towers with white vapour merging with the hazy horizon.

I covered 10km very fast, before I stopped in the woods for a rest. Sitting on a log, in a clearing surrounded by tall mature pines, I spotted a pair of long red socks carefully spread out to dry. Had these been forgotten by another walker in front of me?

I was hungry now after a truly miserable breakfast that morning. As the only guest I was served by an elderly Chinese woman who stood behind me and watched me drink every drop of the small cup of coffee she brought. A request for a second cup was met by an inscrutable oriental stare and a reluctant refill. A well-melted and rehardened bar of chocolate was all I had left and I stopped later by a hedgerow to devour it. Stinging insects drove me on and when I came out of the woods, at the edge of the frontier, a huge autoroute, E25, was barring the way. This was one of the main roads south into France. The traffic flow was unrelenting and the noise thunderous. The GR5 crossed the autoroute by a new footbridge and it was dizzying to stand in the middle and look at the river of vehicles below. As usual the noise died away after a few hundred metres and I walked into the border town of Dudelange by quiet byroads.

This was my seventh day walking since my last day of rest and, since the city of Luxembourg was only a short train ride to the north, it seemed like a good idea to take a break and spend a day there. I had to wait only five minutes for the next train and was into the city in the late afternoon.

14 June

On the previous evening I had gone out to explore the city: the first of any size since Maastricht. I found it incredibly noisy, with speeding cars, squealing tyres and blaring radios. After five weeks of woodland walking, gentle rhythms and long periods of silent contemplation, the contrast was a shock.

The old centre of Luxembourg is the Bock, a gigantic rock plateau surrounded by a deep ravine. A castle, constructed here in the tenth century, developed into one of the most formidable fortifications in Europe. By the nineteenth century the fortress was considered to be a threatening military installation and when Luxembourg gained its independence, as a neutral grand duchy, in 1867, one of the conditions was that the fortifications be demolished. Today only the bases of great bastions, ramparts and parapets survive but beautiful stone-built scarps rise up out of the living sandstone walls of the ravine. The rock is riddled with underground casements; they are now tourist sites, but they served as bomb shelters in the Second World War.

Luxembourg, Bock

The old centre is reached by slender viaducts from the modern city and I walked around the top of the ravine until I found a satisfactory place to sit and draw. Afterwards I climbed down to the bottom of the ravine, a public park, and ended up almost walking the equivalent of an average day. So much for my day of rest!

Map 6: Lorraine

CHAPTER 5

The Plains of Lorraine

15 June

The early train for Dudelange was still at the platform and, although it was a couple of minutes after the displayed departure time, I ran to catch it. There was no time to find a machine to punch my ticket, so I jumped into the nearest carriage, just before the doors closed. I had hardly settled back in my seat when a ticket inspector appeared. He subjected me to a long lecture on the illegalities, if not evils, of omitting to punch my ticket before boarding the train and my explanation of not seeing a machine and of being a mere tourist did not wash. I barely suppressed my rage when he made me pay all over again and, to add insult to injury, fined me 50 francs. His hectoring continued until he moved down the compartment, leaving me for the rest of the journey to try to forget the incident. After about fifteen minutes back on the GR and up on a lovely winding path along a wooded ridge, I simmered down, thoughts pleasantly meshing again to the rhythm of my body.

I was almost bounding along, refreshed after the rest day and excited that within an hour or so I would cross the frontier and be well into France by the evening. Walking through Holland and Belgium had been more interesting than I had expected but I was glad these countries were behind me. France was my Mecca and sojourns there had been a delight ever since that first exhilarating landing at Dieppe 44 years before. Although Hazlitt felt that solitary journeys were not to his liking in foreign parts, because he wanted to hear the sound of his own language occasionally, he made an exception of France:

> *I did not feel this want or craving very pressing once, when I first set my foot on the laughing shores of France. Calais was peopled with novelty and delight. The confused, busy murmur of the place was like oil and wine poured into my ears.*

The route now went through what had once been a vast coal mining area, as the numerous pits and carbonised soil testified, but nature had healed the scars, covering the mounds and hollows with young birches, oaks, pines and hazel trees. I went wrong briefly where one of those silly signs, a yellow triangle where there should have been a yellow disc, sent me down a track towards a village off the route. A gap in a broken fence led into a dense wood and suddenly there was a painted white stripe over red. My beloved GR waymark, last seen on the Belgian frontier eleven days before. I was in France at last!

A cool woodland walk through stands of magnificent tall beeches led out on to open fields of barley, past hedges entwined with wild roses. A long white farm track pointed to the hazy distance and it was now getting very warm – the hottest day so far. I had hoped to get water at the first French village, Escherange, but when I arrived there it seemed deserted. The café was shuttered, a sign stating that it was closed on Mondays, Wednesdays and Fridays and on the other days it did not open until 5.30 p.m. Pushing on, by midday I was parched and not a house in sight. I was getting a bit desperate when I broke out of a strip of woods onto a major road at a pass called Bellevue. The guidebook had no indication of any facilities there but smack in front of me was the most welcome sight. A truckers' mobile café complete with tatty awning, broken tables and scattered plastic chairs. Huge trucks pulled up with air brakes hissing; others roared off in clouds of black diesel. It was hell but I loved it. I downed a litre of bottled water and then settled down under the awning with another litre and a bag of greasy chips. There is something to be said for civilisation.

Sticking a third bottle of water into my rucksack, I set out on the final 10km to the village of Fontoy where the guidebook said there was a hotel. The route was well marked along the side of a wooded valley which ended in a steep forested coombe. The track vanished in a recently felled area and I made repeated forays to find a waymark. After a frustrating half-hour search, I gave up and because, according to the map, Fontoy was on the plateau above, I took a chance and fought my way up through tangled growth until I could break out onto the edge of open ground. In the distance was a church spire. Guessing this must be the correct village, I struck off through the fields. I came on the red and white signs near the first houses and looked for the hotel. No sign of it. Enquiring in a café, I was told by a friendly woman that it was closed but that I could take a bus down the road into the next town of Knutange where there was another.

I approached the village bus stop and saw two walkers. One of them, a tall young woman, turned and said to me, 'Are you the Irishman?'

I was stunned. It was like 'Dr Livingstone I presume?' We introduced ourselves; she was Sandrijn Vink from Utrecht and her companion, Henk, was her father. She had met the Dutch couple, John and Marie, in Vianden and they had told her about me. We must have been walking more or less the same stages for weeks with our paths crossing and recrossing without ever meeting until that evening. She was attempting to walk the GR5 all the way from Maastricht to the Alps, hoping to get as far as possible in the ten weeks she had to spare. Her father had only just joined her for a few days. After such a long lonely day it was a huge boost to meet fellow walkers again and particularly to meet the first 'real' long-distance traveller, like myself, who was attempting to walk most of the route in one go. Knutange was just a few kilometres away and the bus left us outside an old-fashioned hotel where we were warmly welcomed by an elderly woman who showed us to comfortable rooms. It was a large hotel but we seemed to be the only guests, at least in the dining room that night. Dinner was superb. A sausage and noodle dish with crispy bread was so substantial that we thought it was the main course, but then a plate of beef bourguignon arrived, accompanied by bowls of little round deep-fried potatoes. The desert was a delicious light gateau with a meringue topping. With a flask of local wine, the bill was 50 francs each. We wondered was this the celebrated French country cooking we read about in guidebooks? It was certainly my best meal in 36 days and with the friendly hotel and new companions, my spirits were lifted. Any doubts I had about my long-distance goal vanished that night.

16 June

My first day in France inspired an enthusiastic diary entry that the difference between Luxembourg and just a few kilometres into France was striking. The biggest thing is the friendliness. Everywhere I was greeted with *Bonjour, Bon Marche* or *Bon*

Route. Cheerful waves, people pointing me in the right direction and Madame in the hotel really interested in what I was doing. Compared to the indifference of the Luxembourgers, this is a real tonic. The landscape, however, bears the marks of a grim industrial past. Most of the iron ore and coal mining is now gone and the loss to the local economy is evident in the closed or nearly empty hotels and drab buildings where paint peels from façades and rusting balconies.

Madame had to go off early, so this meant a quick breakfast followed by a dash for the first bus. The others managed to catch it but I just missed it and had to wait 30 minutes for the next one back to rejoin the GR at Fontoy. I had been looking forward to at least a day's walk with company and was disappointed to have missed the Dutch couple. In conversation the night before, we had agreed that regular stops for coffee or a cool drink were essential pleasures on long walks and when I arrived at Neuchef, the first village along the trail, I looked into each café I passed. There was no sign of them.

It was another hot day, but the route was mainly through deliciously cool beech woods and soon after leaving the village I turned a corner and saw Sandrijn and Henk sitting on a log. We shared our lunch rolls and chocolate. Sandrijn was 30 and had a stressful job, which she indicated was the main reason for her undertaking the trip. She said she had been given sick leave but I wondered if taking on a couple of thousand kilometres walk with a heavy rucksack would be what any normal doctor would order. I told them about my retirement course medic's advice to walk a couple of miles a day and we each smugly agreed that we were special cases – nut cases! Henk was about 55 and had just retired from the Dutch Air Force. He was looking forward to peaceful country living.

The path through the delightful Bois des Allemand led eventually down a long narrow wooded ravine to the outskirts of the town of Rombas. The waymarks were a real pleasure to follow after the sheer cussedness of the Luxembourg yellow triangles, yellow discs, green triangles and white squares. We were told that we could find a hotel about 2km down the street and duly arrived on the rue de la Gare, which should have been a warning. The Café-Hotel-Restaurant de la Poste was a miniature château-like structure with an aggressive terracotta and cream-painted façade. The small raised terrace had a whitewashed plinth with large black-painted lettering announcing, *'Ici Glaces Maison'*. It looked decidedly down-at-heel but was cheap. We reluctantly took rooms after being assured by the proprietor that the noise of trains, which was ear-splitting, would cease at night. We did not fancy the restaurant in the hotel and went out to eat, but the only place we could find, in that seedy, run-down town, was the equivalent of an ice cream parlour and chip shop. The staff were welcoming but a little surprised that we wanted a sit-down meal and then, to our astonishment, produced a truly mouth-watering steak with peppercorns, fresh haricot beans and a salad. Only my second meal in France on this trip and it was looking good.

17 June
The Hotel de la Poste must come high on the list of weird places. The owner's assurances about the train noise only proved the extent of our gullibility. Trains shunted, banged, roared and squealed all night, both in front and to the rear of the hotel. Sleep was impossible. When we came down for breakfast, Monsieur and Madame were having a flaming row in the lobby, while in the dining room they were noisily setting

up tables for another of those mass, soft-selling exercises; this time it was chinaware. When a coachload of elderly customers pulled up outside, we paid and fled.

Henk went off to the station to catch a train to Holland while Sandrijn set off at a cracking pace up the hill to rejoin the trail. My usual practice was to start slowly and gradually build up a steady rhythm. This time I tried to keep up with her but I was soon left behind. I plodded on for an hour and came out to an area beside a reservoir which had been laid out as an exercise park. Up ahead of me on the forest track I spotted Sandrijn, now walking more slowly and obviously feeling the weight of her heavy rucksack. When I caught up with her, we rested for a while and I tried and failed to pick up her pack. Her explanation for the weight was that she planned to camp for as many nights as possible and so had to carry tent, sleeping bag, cooking utensils and everything but the kitchen sink. I was glad I was older and wiser. After a couple of hours we arrived onto the summit of Drence, our first hill since the Ardennes, although it was only 375m high. A metal tower with a viewing platform on top was above the tree canopy and gave a wonderful panorama; east to the valley of the Moselle and the city of Metz.

The path led out on to the edge of an escarpment where there was a boundary stone dating from the eleventh century. Along the crest Sandrijn forged ahead and disappeared while I kept up my slower but, I hoped, steady pace. After 14km I diverged a short way into the little village of Bronvaux to rest with a cool drink on a shady terrace. The place was so quiet that two little boys were playing with remote controlled toy cars up and down the street and in and out of the legs of the odd pedestrian. The sun got hotter and after I crossed under a motorway and suffered a few kilometres of open country, the heat affected me so much that I had to flop down beside an old stone bridge for a rest. I heard my name being shouted from the hill above and when I climbed up the track, I found Sandrijn sitting under a tree. We had a long rest there in relatively cool shade and talked about the stages ahead. The day was a 26km walk for me – more than enough – and I planned to stop at Saulny and maybe travel into Metz for a night. She resolved to push on a further 9km to a camp site.

The last few kilometres were punishing, on tracks through open fields where strawberries ripened and the sun blazed. Arriving at the village of Saulny was a relief and the shady café with cold drinks was heaven. Sandrijn and I had been more or less together for two days and I think we both came to the unspoken conclusion that we liked each other well enough to continue to meet and perhaps walk together for company. Before we parted we made a tentative arrangement to link up again in two days and after consulting the map fixed on the small town of Pagny-sur-Moselle. This little place was just off the GR and we agreed to meet at the first bar-café or hotel on the way in.

The café proprietor told me that the last bus had left for Metz but that I could find another at Woippy, 3km down towards the river valley. I trudged the hot hard road and then had to wait for over an hour for a bus into the Place d'Armes, the old city centre. I quickly found a pleasant hotel and went out to explore this marvellous ancient city.

The Romans founded Metz and its situation, on the confluence of the Moselle and the Seille, made it one of the most important crossroads of navigable waterways in Europe. The Cathedral of Saint-Etienne is one of those superb examples of French Gothic where the structure is refined and reduced to a tall stone skeleton, infilled with sparkling stained glass. The hotel was in the medieval core with its narrow streets and yellow sandstone buildings. That warm evening was sheer delight.

18 June

My diary entry hinted at my sense of contentment: *I am 40 days out. Not quite 40 days in the desert but certainly days of unusual living. A simple life really, with the only concerns being occasional navigational problems and, at the end of each day, finding a bed.* I missed the 9 a.m. bus which was just as well, since a taxi took me straight back to the GR at Saulny and I avoided the gruelling uphill road trudge from Woippy. It turned out to be even hotter than the previous day and a good deal of the route was on farm tracks and little roads with no shade. The high June sun just scorched down on my head and for some time I needed to wear a hat and to pull the brim down against the intense sky glare.

Shortly after I left Saulny, the waymarks disappeared. A bulldozer was tearing up the track ahead and when I stopped to puzzle out where to go, a man came out of his house and showed me an alternative way to rejoin the route further on. He was right. I crossed a potato field and soon broke through a wide strip of nettles onto the trail again. I was not so lucky at the pretty village of Jussy where I met one of those 'perfidious locals' again. This individual accosted me and proudly announced that he also was a long-distance walker; in fact, the organiser of the local walking fête. He took me by the arm and walked me confidently along a path and pointed out where, according to him, the GR5 went. I was a bit doubtful, as well as wary of confident locals. After ten minutes on the path, it was obviously wrong and I returned to where I had started. The local had vanished but the correct route was in the opposite direction. In fact, 100m from where this character had given me false directions, there was an enormous signboard and map advertising the GR5 through Lorraine! I don't think he was trying to fool me; he was just an idiot.

The final stretch to my night's stop at Ars-sur-Moselle was through cool woods and on a viewpoint above the little town I could see the Moselle and, in the distance, the remnants of the Roman aqueduct. The first hotel I came to was closed on Saturdays, but there was another nearby. All the restaurants in the town were also closed, because of a fête, so I had to settle for a take-away pizza, which I ate in my room.

19 June

Another hot day even at 7.30 a.m., when I started, and it got hotter. So far it had been nearly impossible to arrange an early breakfast in any hotel along the way. The usual times offered were 8 a.m. or even 8.30 and it took some persuasion the night before for the hotel to agree to 7.30. When the weather was as hot as it was that summer, it was imperative to have an early start. This time I managed to get my cup of coffee and two rolls at 7.30 and I was quickly away. The path went past the great Roman aqueduct and I stopped to have a good look at it. The massive structure was built towards the end of the first century AD and carried water from the hill town of Gorze to Metz. The yellow stone arches took the channel over the Moselle for a distance of 1,200 metres and basins at each end collected the water which flowed in an underground conduit from the hills. The 2,000-year-old structure was an impressive landscape feature, just as the modern concrete motorway viaducts are today but I wondered if the ruins of these would still be here after another 2,000 years.

Gorze was a pretty little place seen from the trail, deep in a valley and surrounded by fields of gold-green barley. Even in the shady woods it was hot but as the day wore on, the clouds thickened and there were a few heavy drops of rain and a hint of thunder. I thought before this walk that I would not welcome rain but trudging along drenched in sweat was hell and I relished the thought of a cool downpour. At the little village of Bayonville I passed over an old stone bridge but the route then led onto an unpleasant busy road by a river. On the riverbank, despite the closeness to traffic, were groups of French families – lolling in the heat, drinking wine, indulging noisy children and generally enjoying themselves as I plodded by, feeling sorry for myself. Under a railway bridge I met a large party of French walkers striding along and whistling 'It's a long way to Tipperary'. Responding to their cheerful greetings was hard! A cruel and unrelenting climb up through woods left me exhausted and dripping with sweat. I lay prone on the grass, my shoes off, for a half hour to recover. When I forced myself on, it was distinctly cooler and I hoped that a thunderstorm in the night might break the heatwave.

After a long day and 25km covered, I arrived out on the edge of an escarpment above the river. The town of Pagny-sur-Moselle lay below. Just as I entered the town centre, there was a small hotel and bar-restaurant right on a corner. I booked in, showered and then went to sit in the bar, picking a spot where I could watch up the street for Sandrijn. An hour passed and a familiar figure appeared, bowed under that enormous rucksack. We were reunited under the amused gaze of Monsieur, who never seemed to leave the bar – he just stood there motionless. We asked him if we could have an early breakfast because we both felt that the heat was now too much in the middle of the day. He asked what time did we require? We wondered what would be his earliest offer and he shrugged and replied, '*Huit heures, sept heures, six heures, cinq heures.*' We settled for 6 a.m.

We drank too much wine that night, an excellent Edelswicker from Alsace, stayed up too late and regretted asking for the early morning call.

20 June

We started that morning, first walking through the forest of Sainte-Marie and then out to an open plateau where there was a delicious cool breeze. We ambled along farm tracks through fields of waving barley, dotted with poppies and purple loosestrife. There was a scent of woodbine in the hedges. We stopped often to gorge ourselves on wild strawberries along the way. At one point we took a wrong turning in the woods where the waymarks simply vanished and had to use a compass to get back on the route. Eventually we made it to the village of Vilcey-sur-Trey.

The map here was covered with zigzag serrated lines with names such as Tranchée de la Justice, Tranchée de Fer, Tranchée des Carrières, Tranchée des Princes, Tranchée de la Fontaine Noisette, Tranchée de la Croix Charbonnier. We were in the middle of the Great War battlefield of Bois le Prêtre. From January to August 1915 the French 73rd and 128th divisions lost 29,000 killed and wounded here and, according to the guidebook, the Germans 'probably' had similar casualties. When the newly arrived Americans took over this sector in

August 1918, the opposing trenches were only 20m apart in places. When we stopped for a rest we realised that the grass bank we were sitting on had been the rampart of an old trench and all around us were shell holes with the remnants of rusty barbed wire poking through the grasses and wild flowers. The guidebook warned not to stray from the path because there were still unexploded shells and mines in the woods.

It was a strange and moving experience to sit in silence and try to imagine the massed barbed wire, the mud, the roar of the guns and above all the men who died all around us in thousands. We were only a few miles from Verdun where, possibly, the most awful concentrated slaughter of the whole war took place.

After the Franco-Prussian conflict of 1870, where the French suffered an ignominious defeat at Sedan and lost the provinces of Lorraine and Alsace, it was resolved that never again would the French army give up ground. They would always attack. The infamous, so-called 'strategy' of *L'Attaque à outrance* and the adopted slogan 'They shall not pass' led to the ten-month offensives and counter offensives at Verdun and total casualties, French and German, of over half a million men. It was a Pyrrhic victory for both sides; the French stopped the German advance but the French army was bled dry, as the strategy devised by General von Falkenhayn intended, but with far greater losses to his own army than he expected. The incredible volume of high explosives over a small area has blighted the countryside for generations and it is said that, even today, there is more chance of a small cut being infected here than anywhere else in France.

The region is dotted with war cemeteries and we diverted to visit one: the Cimetière Militaire du Pétant. On a south-facing slope above the river were row upon row of small white crosses, each with a name and the inscription *Mort pour la France*. A single red rose was planted beneath the name. We walked on, mostly in silence, to the town of Montauville, overcome by the sadness of the place.

French First World War cemetery

Pont-à-Mousson, where we planned to spend the night, was only 45 minutes off the trail but our low spirits, combined with tiredness, made us wait at a bus stop for nearly an hour before we could be driven into the town. Walking through the narrow streets, we were attracted by organ music from an old church and on entering were treated to a concert of rich Baroque sounds which brought our spirits back to the joyful present.

21 June

I was now within one day's walk of the city of Nancy. This was where I had planned to meet my next supporter, Sally Keogh, who was flying out from Dublin to accompany me for about six days walking. We had been walking companions for many years but, except for one epic cliff walk in Donegal, I had not been with her on any very long treks. In planning the journey, one of the problems was where and when to meet with each of the friends who had offered support for me at various stages. I had worked out target destinations and arrival days for the whole trip but it was obvious that it was a near impossibility to adhere absolutely to the plan. A walk of a couple of thousand kilometres is too far and too unpredictable for tight timetables and, in any case, all pleasure in the journey would quickly be replaced by extreme anxiety if I became obsessed with keeping to exact targets. One day missed and the programme is redundant.

It was possible, however, to target arrival times within three or four days and applying a little lateral thinking produced the scheme that Sally would get in to Nancy from Paris on 23 June and I would meet her there. If I had not yet reached Nancy on the walk, I would simply go on by bus or train to meet her and we would travel back to rejoin the GR. Similarly, if I was ahead of the target day I would travel back for the meeting place and repeat the exercise. I was now just two days ahead of schedule and the plan looked good. After so many weeks of walking alone, until I had met Sandrijn, I was looking forward to joining up with Sally for the rest of the crossing of Lorraine. The enticing prospect of having someone to share the adventures of the journey often kept me going on long lonely stretches. It seemed that I had abandoned Hazlitt's philosophy, at least temporarily.

The leg from Montauville to Liverdun was, at 29km, one of the longest I had attempted so far. In spite of this, I walked well and fast and kept up with Sandrijn's pace for most of the way. Wild strawberries in the woods seduced us again and we had to discipline ourselves to pick a full handful of the tiny berries before giving in to the delicious taste. When we stopped for lunch along a forest track, we were overtaken by a middle-aged woman in tight, electric-blue running gear. She jogged past without a greeting, pink-faced and sweaty, while a long way behind her was her husband, or so we presumed, somewhat overweight and suffering as he tried to keep up. He slowed to a walk as he passed and we said to him *bon courage*. He gave us a resigned grin and struggled on.

It was another day of scorching sun and powder-blue sky. We went through cornfields speckled with poppies, the larks were still singing and nesting swallows screeched in the eaves of the little villages along the way. A thunder of jet fighters split the calm as we came close to the military airfield of Rosières en Haye. The pilots were practising close take offs and landings in groups of three and the tearing noise followed us all along blindingly white sandy tracks through fields of ripening oats. The day ended in Liverdun, on a high hill with a splendid view down to the wide Moselle and a short distance from Nancy.

The GR5, which had been directly south from the Luxembourg border, now turned sharply east to cross Lorraine to the foot of the Vosges Mountains.

A decision had to made at Liverdun. I was a day early for Sally's arrival in Nancy and I had planned a rest day there with her before setting out to complete the journey across Lorraine. Sandrijn wanted to press on because her time was more limited than mine, so we agreed to walk together for one more day. We decided to use Nancy as a base for a day's walk without rucksacks. This involved travelling into the city, which was 30 minutes by train south of the GR, booking a hotel for two nights and travelling by train or bus back and forth.

We had to wait nearly three hours for the next local train and when a silver TGV howled past without stopping, a grumpy Frenchman complained that since these 'things' arrived the local service had gone from bad to worse. Sitting in a café terrace in the sun and drinking cold beer made the wait more than bearable and we arrived in Nancy in time to book into the friendly Jean Jaures Hotel.

22 June

A day walking without a rucksack. The thought was bliss but the reality was that at first we both felt unbalanced, disoriented and somewhat uneasy. All our possessions had been left behind and we felt giddy when the plodding, top-heavy gait was replaced by this light-hearted scamper. An hour of bounding along swept away the anxiety and we abandoned ourselves to the freedom.

We had to get up early that morning since there was only one train that stopped at Liverdun. We rose at 5.30 and had a fast walk to the station without breakfast. It was our earliest yet on the trail and it felt marvellous to be in the woods on this

June morning. Along the way the cobwebs glistened with dew and brushed our faces as we pushed past overgrown paths. The route went north for a few kilometres initially and crossed La Grande Tranches, another reminder of the First World War. In the early weeks of 1914 the French recklessly plunged against the German-occupied Lorraine, hoping to regain their beloved province, lost in the war of 1870. In uniforms unchanged from that time, blue greatcoats and red trousers, the cavalry wearing shiny brass, plumed, helmets and with bands playing and colours flying, they pushed the Germans back some 30km. Within six days they were driven back by superior forces commanded by Crown Prince Rupprecht, but they finally stopped the German offensive on a line just north of the city of Nancy and here the armies remained for the next four years.

We traversed this high ground, scarred with trenches, and after 9km dropped down to cross the Moselle. The next stage was a long woodland walk through the Bois de Faulx, the tranquillity again shattered by low-flying jet fighters. If that wasn't enough, they were followed by a fleet of clattering military helicopters. Did the French think there was another German invasion?

While walking through one dense patch of woods we encountered a group of young men, army conscripts perhaps, gathered together in a clearing and looking at a map. They looked lost and when they saw us they asked us if we could point out their location on their map. It seems that they had been sent out on an orienteering course for the first time and had not got the foggiest notion of where they were. This was one of my own sports and it didn't take long for me to compare their map with ours and line up the visible features on the ground. I could see that they were not far from one control point and showed them their correct direction. Thanking us they rushed off, charging through the undergrowth like a herd of cattle and breaking all the rules for novice orienteers: think first, then walk off slowly, aligning the map with the direction of travel. We continued on our way and ten minutes later the same bunch burst out of the woods across our track going in a totally different direction. We never saw them again.

The pretty village of Amance was perched on a hill: narrow winding streets and traditional houses of stone and tiled roofs, some with carvings on the façades. There was a thirteenth-century church at the top and the whole place looked carefully preserved. The expensive cars parked outside the houses pointed to a takeover of the village by commuters to Nancy.

We raced the final stage to the village of Brin-sur-Seille at the speed of greyhounds and by three in the afternoon had covered over 30km – a highly satisfactory day. There was no bus from the village, so we phoned for a taxi which arrived after an hour and took us right back to Nancy.

It was a warm evening and we had a meal on an outdoor terrace in the old centre. Sandrijn had decided to leave early the next morning and continue on from where we had left off. I was sorry that we had to say goodbye. We discussed the possibility of meeting again and hoped we would, but since she would have two days start on me, I doubted that I could catch up.

23 June

Sandrijn left at 6.30 to travel back to Brin-sur-Seille and we made our farewells, exchanging addresses and promising that if we didn't meet up again on the trail, we would get in touch afterwards to share stories of our adventures. She strode off in her characteristically strong way and I returned to a leisurely breakfast.

I went out to explore the city, strolling first to the Place Stanislaus. This is a splendid ensemble of the eighteenth century. The serene classical architecture is complemented by the baroque bravura of the fountains by sculptor Guibal and the gold-leaved iron gateways by ironmaster Jean Lamour. The Place is named after the dethroned King of Poland, Stanislaus Leszczynski, who was awarded the province of Lorraine by the Peace of Vienna which, in 1735, followed the War of the Polish Succession. The city is far older, however. The earliest quarter dates from the tenth century and a fine gateway from the fourteenth century remains.

I lingered over coffee on a shady terrace, wrote numerous postcards and then enjoyed a *salade vosgesienne,* anticipating the first real mountains, now almost in my sights. Sally arrived on the early afternoon train from Paris and we greeted each other warmly before settling down to a celebratory glass of wine at another outdoor café, this time for her to enjoy the blazing sun after the dull grey skies of Dublin. I sat in the shade.

Dinner that warm midsummer night was again at an outdoor restaurant and we enjoyed reading the menus and speculating on the specialities of Lorraine. Quiche we knew about but what about that other famous local speciality, *Les Bergomettes de Nancy*? It was just as well we didn't order this delicacy since we discovered later that it was little boiled sweets. They are scented with essence of the herb bergamot and are one of the oldest specialities of Nancy.

24 June

The plan had been to take the first day after Sally's arrival as a rest day. The next stage to the foot of the Vosges had to be planned because this, according to other travellers, was a region where lodgings were scarce. In addition, it was necessary to make sure that Sally's pack and contents were suitable. I thought her rucksack was a disaster. It was very heavy and, in my opinion, she had far too many unnecessary items. We had a small confrontation about this but she soon, if reluctantly, agreed to reduce the weight. I told her about my early torture with a heavy load and advised leaving out everything that wasn't essential. The pack was emptied on the floor and every item was argued over. Nearly half the contents were eventually agreed to be disposable. We arranged to leave these in the hotel and she would break her journey back to Paris to collect them.

I don't think that I was the best of companions that day. Restless and agitated was probably the most accurate way to describe my mood. It was the usual story: rest days made me feel caged and two days in the same place provoked despair that I would ever finish the journey. I would total up the kilometres achieved so far, divide by the number of days on the trail, calculate the distance still to go and then depress myself with the result. Although I had taken only four days off as rest periods up to Nancy, out of 44 since I had started, the restless urge to keep going was becoming an obsession. The clamour of cities did not help; it was too brutal a change from the quiet of the woods and the gentle rhythm along footpaths.

The sublime gardens in the city centre, La Pépinière, were a solace and refuge from the traffic noise and a lazy few hours there helped to heal my restlessness. The 23 hectares of mainly formal gardens include a magnificent collection of tropical plants, bandstands and a zoo.

It was another day of blue skies and scorching sun and was still warm enough in the evening for another outdoor meal. We chose a restaurant on one of the narrow streets which are barred to traffic after 6 p.m. and filled, instead, with white linen-covered tables, each with a candle. Traffic din is replaced with talk and the sound of footsteps on the cobbles.

It was time to move on and I resolved that night not to take another rest day for a long time.

25 June

A fast taxi brought us back to Brin-sur-Seille in an hour. It was hot even at 8.30 when we started on the trail. The landscape was now totally different to the country I had traversed since Luxembourg. The big forests were gone and the walk was now across an open plateau, with rolling cornfields, little rounded knolls crowned with trees, shallow valleys, an occasional tiny hamlet complete with church and spire. It was a quiet walk, since even the small paved roads we used were free of traffic and we saw hardly a soul all day. By 11 a.m. the heat was intense and although we each had two bottles of water, they were already drastically reduced. The mosquitoes were particularly bad, at least in the few wooded sections we passed through. Many of the paths were overgrown and it didn't look as if anybody had been this way for months. The heat was such that we were wearing as little as possible and the long grasses and prickly vegetation scratched our bare arms and legs.

We had our lunch stop out in the open, settling down in the long grasses by the edge of a vast field. This was not by choice, since the sun high overhead was burning hot, but the cooler woods were impossible because of the torment of biting mosquitoes. The route continued along stony tracks, punctuated by apple trees, at the edges of wide fields and, where we could, we stepped from shade to shade, bracing ourselves for the roasting whenever we had to cross the open spaces again. We passed through the tiny villages of Grémecey and Salonnes where windows and doors were all shuttered and silent in the heat.

Our destination was the little town of Vic-sur-Seille. I reasoned that a 20km stage would be more than enough for Sally on her first day. In the end she had no trouble at all with the distance, except for the heat, thus disproving the sexist admonition of Robert Louis Stevenson who felt that on a walking tour: *you must have your own pace, and neither trot alongside a champion walker, nor mince in time with a girl.* My female fellow walkers so far had all walked, sometimes to my chagrin, better than me. The author of *Virginbus Puerisque,* from which this gem is quoted, and pioneer of the long distance trail in France as told in *Travels with a Donkey* did have some sensible advice, however, for the long distance venturer:

> *There should be no cackle of voices at your elbow, to jar on the meditative silence of the morning. And so long as a man is reasoning he cannot surrender himself to that fine intoxication that comes of much motion in the open air, that begins in a sort of dazzle and sluggishness of the brain, and ends in a peace that passes comprehension.*

The guidebook indicated a hotel in Vic-sur-Seille but when we entered the town we were told at a little café that it was closed and that the nearest place to stay was in Château-Salins, 6km north of the GR. Sally was downcast because I had encouraged her that this was where we would stop. From experience, I knew how bitter the thought of any extra distance is when the enticing prospect of a cool beer followed by a shower and a comfortable bed is frustrated. I told her that we would just phone for a taxi and sit down with a drink while we waited. She was relieved that I was not such a dedicated masochist that I would march every step of the way off route.

We had hardly finished our drink when the taxi arrived and the cheerful driver told us how this whole area was suffering a decline and that all the farmland was now owned by a handful of farmers, hence the nearly empty countryside. He told us about a fête in the town that night and when he deposited us at the hotel in Château-Salins he said he would pick us up in the morning and take us back to the trail. Everybody in the old-fashioned hotel was friendly and interested in us and I certainly loved the contrast of the warm welcome here to the indifference further north.

On our way to the centre for the fête, we encountered the other attraction of the evening – a visit by a 'famous' pop group. We had never heard of them. They were in a huge American convertible, a classic 1960s' model complete with fighter tail fins and acres of chrome. In the square an enormous pile of wood stood ready for the bonfire while youths enthusiastically threw firecrackers. A thunderstorm broke with a deluge which prevented the fire being lit and we trailed back to the hotel along with the drenched revellers. There was a spectacular display of lightning that night.

26 June

The morning dawned with a rain-washed sky and it was distinctly cooler. Our friendly taxi driver arrived promptly and drove us back to the trail at Vic-sur-Seille. He spoke again about the breakdown in village life in this part of Lorraine; the failure of the small farm, and the three families who now own all of the land in the region. The small farm evidently had little future in the new European Union.

We rejoined the GR and the cooler morning allowed us to walk far and fast in the first few hours. The trail went right through the beautiful and astonishing fortified village of Marsal. We passed over a wooden drawbridge to enter through the twin arches of the magnificent town gatehouse into the square. The village was arranged around a saltworks and the production of this essential commodity had been protected by the kings of France and subject to strict laws and taxation. The gatehouse, designed like a château, and the plain stone industrial buildings were the work of the celebrated military

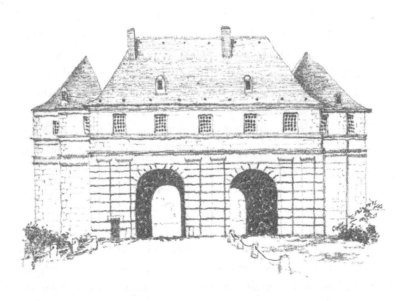

Marsal: the town gatehouse

engineer, Sebastien Leprestre de Vauban, born in 1633. Louis XIV's penchant for wars made necessary the construction of a vast array of fortified towns and other strongholds around the borders of France. Vauban was responsible for the design and construction of most of these and many survive.

We sat for a while in the square, glad to be in the shade but soon it was time to move on, back into the blazing sun and then along a quiet track which went due east – straight for the Vosges. In the sleepy village of Blanche-Église everything was quiet; it seemed that the whole region was untouched by tourism. Each of the handful of people we met that day greeted us warmly, engaged in conversation, and it was obvious that we were rare birds of passage. The Chemin Noir gave us a view of the Étang de Landre, the first lake of any size I had seen for a long time.

Our destination that evening was the Château d'Alteville, a place which was so highly recommended by the American authors of the Sierra guide that we had to try it ourselves. Unusually for Lorraine and, indeed, for the whole route so far, the building was right on the line of the GR5. We had made a phone booking the previous night to the owner, Monsieur Barthelemy, and he had said we would be very welcome.

We were nearly at the end of our tether with the heat and thirst when the gateway to the Château appeared. Standing outside was a relaxed figure smoking a cigar. Monsieur himself was waiting for us to arrive. He took our rucksacks and, ignoring our protestations of being too sweaty and dusty, swept us into the grand salon where we were treated to glasses of ice-cold beer. What a reception! When we recovered, we were shown to the suite of huge rooms on the top floor where we had two bathrooms and long elegant windows looking over the gardens. Château d'Alteville is a late Renaissance house as well as as a fully working farm and Livier Barthelemy has made the mansion into a high-class *gîte rural,* capable of being used for conferences, receptions and as a splendidly luxurious hotel. Dinner that night was with the family, including Monsieur and Madame Barthelemy, and two Czech artists who were restoring an enormous oil painting of a Napoleonic battle scene, one of a pair which hung in the grand salon. The meal was superb. Many of the ingredients came from the farm which was part of the estate. Dessert was a delectable iced chocolate cake drenched in cointreau and followed by coffee in the *petit salon.* We talked, mainly in French, until late.

27 June

When we came down for breakfast early, a rich spread was laid out for us on the antique dining room table. Madame and Monsieur joined us for breakfast. He told us that he was travelling on business in the same direction as us and would transport our rucksacks, thus giving us a day free of carrying. Furthermore, he said that the hotel in the village where we planned to stay that night was closed and that he would book us into another in the nearby village of Heming where the proprietress was a friend. He then told us about the famous stained-glass window by Chagall in the town of Sarrebourg and the newly installed great tapestry there by the same artist. He offered to pick us up at the hotel later in the afternoon and take us to see these. We gladly accepted, overwhelmed by our host's generosity.

We set off on a misty morning but it was already becoming uncomfortably hot. This was the tenth day of a heat wave and it was now humid as well. There were clouds of mosquitoes along the way and Sally got badly bitten. I seemed to escape the worst and thought that I was becoming immune or that the little monsters did not reckon me to be such a succulent target any more.

The landscape was very different now: mainly flat and agricultural with paths along canals and by still lakes bordered by reed beds. A humid heat haze floated over everything and not a breeze stirred. The last stage of the day was a horrible 6km trudge on a hard path, straight along the Canal des Houilères and into the village of Gondrexange.

We were faced here with a more than 3km walk to Heming which was off the route and, worse, along a busy road with speeding traffic. It started to rain heavily as we turned onto the highway, cars and trucks tearing past and showering us in spray. When one hooted at us, we almost gave him the fingers up but it slowed to a stop and reversed. It was Monsieur Barthelemy. We were off the GR now and had no compunction in accepting a lift. He took us straight to the hotel which he had arranged to be opened for us, since on Mondays it was closed until 6 p.m. The elderly proprietress fussed around us and made sure we had everything we needed. Monsieur Barthelemy waited while we had quick showers and then rushed us off to Sarrebourg.

Chagall's window was set in an ancient church and, even though it was a cloudy evening the brilliant colours, so typical of the artist, were spectacular. The glory of the place, however, was the great tapestry, only just completed, where the child-like figures and sumptuous colours translated even better to the soft textures of wool. The Russian-born Chagall designed this work only a short time before he died and this small city of Sarrebourg, population 15,000, commissioned the weaving of the tapestry at the cost of five million francs, nine years after his death. This generous recognition of modern art reminded me of another French city, Angers on the Loire, where the artist Jean Lurçat was celebrated by the bequest of a similar old building for the permanent display of his glorious series of tapestries, entitled 'Song of the World', completed in 1964.

We had a farewell drink with that most amiable of French gentlemen, Livier Barthelemy, telling him that our short stay with him had been truly memorable.

28 June

The thunderstorm of the previous night did little to clear the air and the day grew murkier and as hot as ever. We had to walk back over 3km to rejoin the GR, but fortunately it was along a quiet country road. The guidebook promised a first view of the Vosges mountains when we came out of the wood, Bois de la Minière, but when we reached it we could see nothing but layers of misty gloom. The rolling countryside up to here, however, now gave way abruptly to a different landscape: deep wooded valleys and slopes, tall stands of pine and spruce, Alpine-style villages – the foothills of a mountain range. At the edge of a forest clearing a prominent beech tree was marked with the familiar red and white stripes but also bearing a sign with an arrow pointing back the way we had come and marked 'Holland GR5'.

It was the 1,000km mark and I had now been on the trail for 50 days. This was definitely a milestone for celebration. We took photographs. I felt confident now that I could finish the journey. My obsession with numbers and daily averages took over and I calculated that 20km a day, which was higher if I excluded the rest days, was still on target for me to reach Nice before the first snows fell in the southern Alps.

Saint-Quirin

The path dropped into a deep valley and the beautiful village of Saint-Quirin, dominated by a honey-coloured eighteenth-century church with spires, onion-shaped domes and a classical front. A roadside restaurant here supplied delicious fresh orange juice. Earlier we had stopped at a rough-looking bar-café and were reluctantly served by a strangely menacing, silent man whose arms and all visible skin surfaces were covered in tattoos. He never spoke a word, just watched us closely and when we shortly afterwards branched off into the woods again, we walked fast but occasionally glanced back. I suppose we had read too many newspaper reports of mad axe-murderers lurking in the forest!

There had been few, if any, problems with the route-marking for several days now and we were lulled into a false sense of security. In the forest the path we were following got narrower and narrower and we realised that we had not seen a waymark for ages. Back we went but the only sign we saw was one of those rare GR marks which have the usual red and white stripes but crossed by a white X which means 'wrong way'. This wasn't much use since there were no 'right way' signs. Blundering around for a while we were relieved to spot red and white bands on a small branch and the way soon led steeply uphill into a majestic pine forest and onto the edge of an escarpment, below which we could glimpse the village of Abreschviller – our destination for the day. A steeply winding track led down to the centre where we found a pleasant Logis de France hotel right on the route.

29 June

My first day in the mountains and I loved it. From now on it was up and down all the way to the Mediterranean. We had no sooner left the village than the route climbed steeply through long grasses, yellow broom and tangled briars into a glorious forest of huge firs. It wasn't long, however, before the way-marking began to play games. The Sierra guide had warned of the vagaries of the waymarking system in the Vosges where the local mountaineering organisation, the Club Vosgien, had responsibility. Instead of the familiar red and white stripes, the GR5 was marked by a red rectangle on a larger white rectangle or, at times, a disc. It appears that the club had laid out its route down the crest of the Vosges mountains before the rest of the long distance route, so I suppose it was justified, but for someone walking all the way from sea to sea it is surely more reassuring to have a simple and consistent system.

The middle part of the day's walk was gently but inexorably upwards, sometimes on soft sandy tracks amongst majestic firs and then along cool grassy paths. This was so invigorating after the heavy humidity and scorching sun of the lower plains. We became more confident of the new way-marking when we discovered that the main junctions had prominent signposts labelled Le Donon or GR5. Much of this route upwards followed what must have been the old Roman road across the Col de Donon since the track was punctuated by 'milestones' or *pierre milliaire romaine* at regular intervals. These were carefully squared monoliths of sandstone and seemingly marked the boundaries of responsibility for various commanders or governors.

We emerged from the tall trees onto a high crest and suddenly facing us was Le Donon – the first real summit. Although its forested cone did not look very spectacular, it awakened my infatuations with high places. I was eager to get to the top. The day got hotter but the air was exhilarating up at the Col de l'Engin and a wide view opened up of forested hills and valleys. A punishingly steep climb for 30 minutes led us out on to the summit which at 1,009m was by far the highest point yet reached on my trek. I reflected on the minus altitude back in Holland and, looking out on the vast, dark green, rolling masses of the Vosges, I was confronted with the fact that after I had traversed these, I still had the Jura and then the French Alps to cross. All in good time, I thought, as we lazed here on the summit, particularly relishing the prospect of cold beers down at the Col de Donon where we could clearly see the hotel, our evening's destination.

The panorama from the summit was spectacular. Le Donon was obviously of great significance to the Romans, who built temples near the top. Around the ruins of one was a half circle of upright stones, each with a carved figure of a god or goddess.

The route down to the col was badly marked and we met several perplexed French walkers trying to find their way to the summit. It was satisfying to set them on the right trail upwards and, although we had to guess our way down through a maze of interlocking little paths, we eventually emerged at exactly the correct point on the main road over the col. The hotel was a few hundred metres along and we headed to the shady terrace at full tilt, ordering beers even before we had checked in.

Sally had to make a decision here about when to return. She had found the climb quite hard and was happy to finish on this high note. We were chatting with an amiable English couple on the terrace and when they said that they were driving to Strasbourg the next morning and would be happy to give Sally a lift, she gladly accepted. At dinner that night we celebrated the end of our shared journey across Lorraine, while I resigned myself to the resumption of my solitary status.

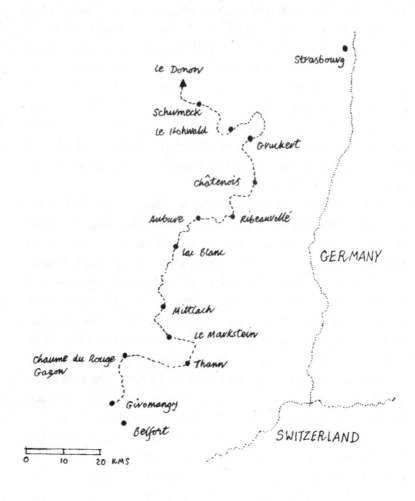

Map 7: Vosges

CHAPTER 6

The Crest of the Vosges

30 June

The Vosges mountains form a natural barrier between France and Germany. After the German victory in the war of 1871, the crest of the range formed the frontier between the two nations. The province of Alsace, as well as Lorraine, were German possessions until the end of the First World War and indeed for the duration of that conflict the front line extended down the crest of the Vosges. My next stage took me down nearly the whole length of that battlefront.

I calculated that the 270km or so of the Vosges section would take me about twelve days, if I did not have a rest day. The frustration of the two days stop in Nancy had made me impatient to keep moving and I resolved to walk to Lac Léman without another stopover. My spirits were low. I was not looking forward to walking alone again. I wondered if I would catch up with Sandrijn but doubted it, knowing her pace.

In this gloomy mood I rejoined the GR where it went downhill through thick woods. The changed waymarking immediately gave me problems because the single dark red stripe, now without a white background, was almost invisible in the cavernous forest. Another problem was that I was now entering serious walking country and the maps were covered with a bewildering maze of waymarked trails crossing and recrossing each other. Every junction had to be carefully checked to keep to the GR5, particularly in dense woods where there were no distant landmarks to reassure me. At one small clearing in the dark woods I met a lone Frenchman picking mushrooms. When I stopped to ask him about his finds, he showed me the tiny yellow ones he had in his basket. These, he said, authoritatively, were quite delicious. I believed him, since the French seem to eat everything that grows and I reflected that nobody at home appears to search for food in the wild anymore. Everything must come in a packet or jar.

Even in the shade of the forest it was hot and when I arrived in the little town of Schirmeck, a café offered a rest from the heat. There was a map of France on the wall and I idly glanced at it, noting with amusement that the mapmakers did not show anything beyond the borders of their beloved country. France was depicted as an island! My amusement turned to disbelief when I saw that I was still only about 20mm from the top right corner of France with at least a straight line distance of 400mm still to go and if the meandering route through the Vosges was typical, then I could double that to Nice. My fourteen-day trek across Lorraine seemed to be for nothing, let alone the earlier 38 days since the North Sea.

I was devastated by this revelation and combined with the effect of murky heat, decided to make a stop at Schirmeck. The fact that there was still 24km before there was anywhere to stay confirmed me in this decision. I went out to search for the hotel but, as so often in weeks past, found not just locked doors but the peeling paint and neglect of a long-closed establishment. I went back to enquire at the café where I was told about the nearby *chambre d'hote* and introduced to the owner. This diffident individual quoted me 150 francs for his studio apartment, which turned out to be a funereal, lower ground floor box of a place with a single bare bulb hanging from a dirty ceiling. I was too tired to protest and too despondent to just go out for a taxi for somewhere better. It was at least cool and I lay on the bed to discover that the place smelt and the nylon sheets looked used. The shower had a broken concrete floor and the hot water was only barely warm. I resolved to go to bed early, get up at 5.30 a.m. and leave immediately. Cheered up by this resolution, I went out to a supermarket and bought a large bag of fruit for breakfast and for the trail.

The main restaurant in the town was shut, so I ate in the local Chinese and drank a bottle of wine, thus dulling my senses in the odiferous bed that night.

1 July

I woke at 5.45 a.m. and had a cold shower. There was no hot water. Breakfasting quickly on half a melon with bread and cheese, I fled from the squalid dump. The night had been noisy with continuous truck traffic on the road to Strasbourg, but ten minutes into the woods and it was quiet. Even as early as this the day promised more humid heat and within an hour I was dripping. My rucksack weighed a ton with all the extra food I had bought so I resolved to eat the apples as I walked.

The path emerged out on a ridge and I arrived at Struthof, the Nazi death camp, where over 30,000 people were exterminated between 1940 and 1945.

I stood to gaze at this terrible place. The double lines of high, barbed wire fences ran down the slope, returning to form a great rectangle. Above the gate was the slogan *Arbeit macht Frie*. The millions of 'undesirables' who entered for slaughter under such arches throughout the Third Reich were greeted by this cruel mockery that work would make them free. Only one line of wooden huts had been preserved; the foundation pads of the others were laid out in the coldly efficient plan of the oppressors. The black gibbet still stood in the centre, a handcart beside it in which inmates were forced to carry off the bodies of those strangled. The worst horror for me was to come.

A few hundred metres down the slope, hidden in the trees, was a small building with a slated roof and neatly carved stone lintels and jambs to the small windows. It looked like a simple Alpine chalet, but when I saw the iron shutters on the inside of the windows I realised that I was looking at the gas chamber. I visualised the lines of broken, half-starved figures being driven down the path from the camp and herded into the dark to die. If it was the summer, as it was when I stood there, they would have walked by wild flowers and the birds would have been singing as they were now, despite all that happened here. How could anyone do this I thought, but then it dawned on me that an architect, one of my own profession, had drawn those pretty windows on paper and worked out the most efficacious hinges and bolts for the iron shutters to resist the clawing fingers.

This concentration camp was built by Heinrich Himmler just after the Germans reoccupied Alsace and although many Jews were amongst those murdered here, the camp was also used to exterminate French Resistance fighters, gypsies, homosexuals, Polish and Russian slave workers and male and female British agents. Possibly the most horrible and evil aspect of the camp was that the commander, Joseph Kramer, had a contract to supply Professor Hirt of the University of Strasbourg with the dead bodies of different racial types for his biological experiments. Kramer performed the gassing himself and was later 'promoted' to commandant of Belsen. He was hanged by the British in 1945.

Staring from outside the barbed wire fence, I could not bear to step inside those gates. I was more shaken by this hideous place than I ever remember and asked myself what kind of monsters could build it here, high up on such a lovely wooded ridge in the clean mountain air?

As I walked away, I thought that I would never shake off what I had seen. The remainder of the trail was through fields of Alpine grasses, by stands of purple foxgloves and past a delightful waterfall or *joli cascade*, as it was signposted. The track wound down to a valley until it emerged abruptly into the village of Le Howald. Right on the route was another *Logis de France* hotel and I was shown into a pleasant if austere room at the rear with French doors opening onto a shady garden. I lay on the bed, the white muslin curtains billowing slightly in a gentle breeze and tried to let the horror of the morning slip away.

2 July
A day that started so well but turned into an epic is my first entry in the diary. The day's stage to Andlau was 25km long but circumstances decided otherwise. I walked fast and strongly despite the fact that it just got hotter and hotter as the sun rose high. The route took another big detour by turning back north to pass the convent of Mont-Sainte-Odile. I could see that by striking east through the woods, I could cut almost

an hour off the stage. There was the distinct possibility of missing the GR5, however, because, according to the new large-scale map, which I had just bought, there was a maze of other walking routes. I plodded on, following the single red stripes which were now familiar and regularly spaced. The paths up to the convent were beautifully graded, contouring ravines but edging gently upwards through cool shade until they led me out onto the summit where the buildings were perched.

I sat at a table in the courtyard, drinking lemonade and watching 30 or more elderly people at a long table tucking into that most serious of meals, a French lunch – at 11 a.m. At the end of the day's stage I would have passed the halfway mark of the long walk. I had mixed feelings about this. After 1,000km, the distance to Nice was getting shorter every day but then: 'My God – do I have to walk another 1,000 plus?' My penchant for rationalisation then soothed me when I worked out that I was only 22 days from Lac Léman and a good break. It now seemed so easy, but then I remembered that map of France back in the hellhole of Schirmeck. I was driving myself mad. It was time to move on.

A glorious long and winding woodland path brought me straight down to the little town of Barr and I was now on the eastern side of the Vosges with the plain of Alsace just below. The town was smouldering in a heat haze and when I emerged from the woods it was into an oven. An hour's walk led to Andlau, along a road and without a sliver of shade. Pulling my hat brim over my eyes, I plodded on with the sun like a hammer on my head and reflected heat burning up from the highway. The map showed this as part of the *Route du Vin* and on both sides regular ranks of vines were forming a carpet of green on the slopes. I wondered if the drivers of the few cars that passed had been sampling at the numerous vineyards along the way.

I was relieved to see hotel after hotel in Andlau, and looked forward to a shower, relief from the heat and rest for my burning feet. At the tourist office I was shocked to find that there was not a bed to be had that night because a town fête was in progress. The helpful young woman was sympathetic and suggested that I continue on to Gruckert where there was a refuge run by the *Amis de la Nature*. The problem was that this place was over an hour away and halfway up a mountain. I was dog-tired and drained from the heat and the prospect of the ordeal continuing nearly finished me. There was nothing to do except go on, however, so I found a shop where I could get some provisions because there were no meals supplied at the refuge. I faced into the 4km slog steeply uphill, brushing clouds of insects away from my face and feeling the damp patch on my back getting wetter. It was my worst experience of the journey so far and the sight of the ramshackle refuge was like a vision of heaven. I had been nine hours on the trail.

Half a dozen walkers were in residence, although no one was doing the GR5, and they made me cheerfully welcome. I had a shower, cooked my tin of stew and had a banana for dessert. One of the company produced bottles of the local wine, a Rosé d'Alsace, and we all swapped stories of walks and life, before retiring to the communal dormitory where even the lumpy mattresses could not keep me from oblivion.

3 July

The temperature was 23° at 6 a.m. I made coffee in the deserted kitchen and went off at seven. After only fifteen minutes on the track I was sweating, even though I was still in the shade of the trees. A short steep climb brought me onto the beautiful summit of the Ungersberg mountain into a deliciously cool breeze. The cairn had a pole on top and stuck on to the side was a folded piece of paper with my name written on it. The note was from Sandrijn! It was a huge surprise and a pleasure, but when I read her message it told me that she was now three days ahead. It would be hard for me to catch up. I was hoping that we could walk the section through the Jura mountain range together but it was not to be. Later I heard that she had abandoned the walk at the end of the Vosges, a combination of tiredness and loneliness made her give up at Belfort.

It was getting hotter but mercifully the trail was mostly in the deep shade of beautiful beech trees. The hills were shimmering in a haze and I could see to the east the table-flat plain of Alsace stretching to the Rhine. The horizon was dissolved in a bluish mist and the outlines of the little medieval villages dotted on the plain were blurred with the heat. It was a long leg to walk and I began to break it up with stops to drink water. I was carrying one litre but it was not nearly enough because I was now drinking three litres a day, so had to ration my intake.

On long sections like this I fell into my usual daydreaming and said to myself that this journey was becoming a way of life. I wondered would there be life after it, since life before it seemed so far away – as far away as the ice-cold North Sea. I felt I would die for the pleasure of plunging into it now.

The ruined fortified château, Berstein, was the first of many on the eastern flanks of the Vosges. The tall pentagonal keep dominated the top of these steep slopes and dated from the Thirty Years War. The path zigzagged steeply down and emerged onto a roadway and the plain at the foot of the mountains. Having started so early and walked so fast, I had covered 23km and was only 30 minutes from the town of Châtenois, where I planned to spend the night. It was lunch-time and an attractive restaurant with a vine-covered terrace seduced me to linger over a long lunch. The place was crowded with French enjoying their national pastime – eating – and I willingly joined them. A salad of smoked trout with two large bottles of mineral water made it easier to sit back and lazily try some of the local wine. Several years before, Nuala and I and a friend, Cathie Hayes, had discovered the pleasures of the white wines of Alsace on a drive up from the south. The splendid Pinot Blanc had been a favourite then and I sampled some now, although I knew it would cause problems when I went back out into the hot sun. Who cared – that was one of the precious luxuries of being alone.

At the entrance to the town there was sign for a *chambre d'hote,* which turned out to be a suburban house. I booked in at once, a wise move since the tourist season had well and truly begun. I had dinner in the town centre and went back early to bed. My room was on the top floor, under the roof, and was baking hot. Even lying naked, windows open, without even a sheet over me, I was slick with sweat and hardly slept.

4 July
All the people at the breakfast table were German car tourists; they had little comprehension of the pleasures of walking. After the previous restless night I felt poorly until I was a long way up in the forest, where the altitude reduced some of the heat and humidity. When I crested a small ridge, a clearing gave me a stunning view of the restored great castle of Haut-

Haut-Koenigsbourg, Vosges

Koenigsbourg. Its stone walls rose sheer from the edges of a high, steep and narrow spur which commanded a superb defensive position. The earliest castle dates from the medieval period; it lasted until it was attacked and wrecked by the Swedes in 1633.

The courtyard was packed with noisy visitors and I slipped back into the quiet woods. An easy downhill walk led me into the pretty village of Thannenkirch where I spotted a cool arbour outside a little hotel. Unfortunately, being Monday, the restaurant was closed so I had to settle for a rest in the shade. Relaxing under the canopy of vine foliage, I became aware of rhythmic sounds nearby. I turned to look for the source and there, hidden in the deep shade at the rear of the arbour, was a hammock containing a fat man in shorts. The sounds were his snores as his round belly rose and fell. Beside him on a table were several empty beer bottles. This picture of contented slumber made me think. What the hell was I doing? He was the one with sense. I slung the awful rucksack up on my back and stepped out into the burning heat, thinking 'mad dogs and Englishmen' – in this case an Irishman – 'go out in the midday sun'.

The heat was cruel and I seemed to take ages to reach the ruined château of Haut-Ribeaupierre where there was a chance to sit in the shade. A single tall tower remains and a steep staircase leads out on top to a spectacular view; eastwards to the plains of Alsace and west and south to the rolling crests of the Vosges. A steep path snaked down through beech woods to another ruined castle, the château of Saint-Ulrich, perched on a spur above the town of Ribeauvillé.

This was a place I had been to on that visit to Alsace several years before. One of the aims of the car journey was to reconnoitre some of the areas I would have to go through on my long walk. I was determined then not to actually walk any part of the GR5 in advance because it would spoil the adventure. When we arrived in Ribeauvillé, however, we were intrigued by the sight of the castle high above the town and could not resist the path up to Saint-Ulrich. This 30-minute track was the only piece of the GR5 I had been on before, but I barely remembered it as I dropped quickly down into the narrow main street.

After finding a hotel, I went to seek out the tourist office fearing that, in high summer, the mountain refuges and hotels might be heavily booked. I managed to reserve rooms for two nights ahead and retired to a shady terrace to drink cold beer and write postcards. This was the hottest day so far and the temperature was in the mid-30s. My room was so hot that it was impossible to sleep and I heard the church clock chime the hours and quarters until the early dawn when I finally dropped off.

5 July

I woke at 6.30 as usual and after a shower went to sit outside in the cool of the terrace. The breakfast was one of the meanest so far: a single croissant, three tiny bits of bread and a cup of coffee. I asked for a second cup and was charged 8 francs extra. Pretty this town may be, but its crooked streets, timber balconies and shops packed with tourist kitsch had more than a feel of Disneyland. The prices and indifferent service added a sour note.

The day's stage was to be a short one, just 14km, but involved a climb of 670m back up towards the centre of the mountain range. As I started to climb the track out of the town, I glanced back and saw two walkers behind me. Only one had a rucksack, a small one, so I expected them to catch up swiftly;

Château Saint-Ulrich

my usual pattern was to start slowly and maintain a steady even pace. Other walkers often passed me, charging along, only for me to catch up later as they sat for rests. The path led relentlessly uphill but after a while I became aware that it was not quite as hot as on previous days. There were satisfactory clouds building up to the east and the higher I got, the cooler it became. A sharp final climb brought me out to the summit rocks – *rocher du Koenigsstuhl* – where I flopped down to enjoy a stretch, *sans* rucksack. After a few minutes the two men joined me on the summit and sat down for a chat.

They were from Holland and were walking a few stages of the GR5, but with the difference that their rucksacks were transported each day to the next place to stay. They shortly moved on, inviting me to have a drink with them at Aubure while I, having plenty of time, dozed off in the shade of the rocks. It was a rollercoaster trail down and up again into the mountain village of Aubure. The two Dutchmen were sitting at the first café on the way in. They ordered a large glass of beer for me and we toasted our efforts on the trail. Sitting under a shady awning, it was good for me to be able to talk English again and to enjoy male banter. We shared our ages – one of them was 48 and the other 62; the younger was amazed at my walk so far and offered to buy me more beer. I protested that I had a kilometre or two yet to walk but they said that they still had two hours to go and that the main reason they went mountain walking was to drink lots of beer! A monumental drinking session was developing and I managed to extricate myself only with difficulty.

I staggered out onto the road and uphill to where my hotel for the night was located high on a pass. It turned out to be a plain concrete block structure with a slightly seedy air. The proprietress seemed surprised at my request for a room notwithstanding the fact that I had booked. The mystery deepened later! There appeared to be nobody else staying despite the numerous tourists around; just a few silent men drinking at the bar. My room, on the upper floor, had a large bed which sagged in the middle, a huge, ancient and broken television and, over the bed, a reproduction of Goya's 'Naked Maja'. Madame then informed me that there was no bathroom but that I could use the shower in another room. This was a bigger space with a crude shower cabinet plonked against one wall, but the real eye-opener was the huge mural painted behind the vast, unmade bed – a full-sized copy of Botticelli's 'The Birth of Venus'.

What kind of a place was this, I asked myself and then, in the corridor, noticed a gigantic dog – a kind of boxer – sleeping in an enormous basket at the head of the stairs.

I had dinner in the ground-floor restaurant and there were only two others eating there, an elderly couple, while the same group of silent drinkers were still at the bar. I took a while to get to sleep, not helped by hearing the dog padding up and down the corridor. Later, to my consternation, I needed to go to the toilet at the other end of the corridor. I lay there for a while wondering what the dog would do if I suddenly appeared but then, unable to hold out any longer I softly opened the door and crept down to the facility. The dog never stirred and I thankfully made it back to bed.

6 July

The previous evening I had asked for breakfast at 7.30 a.m. but this appeared to cause huge difficulty. After dinner, however, Madame informed me that she had arranged that a 'Monsieur' would serve me. When I went to take my morning shower with 'Venus' the room was locked; there was nobody about and the huge slobbering boxer eyed me as he patrolled the corridor. I went down to the bar where I found a sullen young man who silently served me a breakfast which was not worth waiting for.

I was off before eight. It was far cooler now and I walked strongly, even though the climbing was relentless, bringing me up to the highest point yet, Grand Brézouard at 1,228m. Unfortunately most of this height gain was lost when the trail descended to the village of Le Bonhomme. After four hours of almost non-stop walking, I was glad to sit down for a lemonade at a corner café. I was hardly settled when two young Frenchmen, with large rucksacks, sat down at the next table. We got into conversation and I thus met my first longdistance walkers of the GR5 since Sandrijn. They had started from Strasbourg and planned to walk the length of the Vosges and Jura to Mont Blanc. Françoise and Cristophe were students at Strasbourg University and had walked the Kerry Way two years before. They were mostly camping, walking fast and covering greater distances each day than I was, so I felt it was unlikely that I would see them again.

The final three hours of the day's stage was steeply up to the Roche du Corbeau and then on to the summit of the Tête des Faux. This was the site of one of the most terrible battles of the Vosges front in 1914/1915 and the reminders of it were all around me. I walked a path which was red with the rust of barbed wire while great coils of the stuff filled shell holes on each side. The opposing troops were only metres apart. While the French line seemed to consist of trenches and pits, the Germans had constructed one of the most elaborate defensive lines of the whole Western Front. Concrete and stone machine gun nests clustered on their side and a 1,100m, near-vertical, tunnel had been cut into the mountain to supply the forces on the summit. There were wildflowers growing everywhere now: purple loosestrife, meadowsweet, foxgloves and tall grasses filled the no-man's-land but, standing there in the stillness, I could picture the torn mountaintop ravaged by the lines of earthworks, iron posts and tangled wire. As I went down the far side of the mountain, I reflected that these trenches had stretched for nearly 800km, from the North Sea to the borders of Switzerland.

Arriving at the Col du Calvaire du Lac Blanc, I could see the lake which, despite its name, was inky black and lay in the deep shade of a steep slope under the crest of the Gazon du Faing. The refuge du Blancrupt was a modern Alpine-style structure in timber and stone and provided cheap, clean and pleasant accommodation. My meal was a typical Alsacienne dish mainly of sausage, black beans and uneatable thick fatty bacon.

7 July

The previous night was almost cold. I slept for the first time in weeks with a blanket and had a dormitory with seven beds all to myself. Starting out early, full of strength, I had my best day's walking of the whole trip so far. I stormed up the steep wooded slope from the col onto the arête of the Gazon du Faing – the old frontier between France and Germany and the real crest of the Vosges. To the east the ground dropped away steeply to lakes and wooded valleys, while my new view to the west and south was of open grasslands and heaths. The trail ahead gave fabulous walking, springy turf, alpine flowers and larks singing. I thought of Hazlitt again and his delight in the 'lone heaths' where: 'I laugh, I run, I leap, I sing for joy'. I laughed and sang and almost ran, but leaping was difficult with my rucksack. The cold fresh mountain air, at 1,300m, made me feel nearly drunk. I felt as fit as I was 30 years before.

The route led south all along the arête which gradually developed into the lip of an escarpment with dramatic views down steep slopes and vertical cliffs. This glorious path was three hours long but since all good things must end, the horrible Col de la Schlucht was like a slap in the face. A crossroads with roaring traffic, hotels, restaurants, ski-lifts and tacky souvenir shops, it was a scab on the mountain. I had to run between the trucks to get back up the slope, where the noise died away. There were far more people now, hundreds in fact, all heading for the summit of Le Hohneck which, at an hour's walk from the col, was a tourist honeypot. The top, at 1,362m, was another highest point reached and I saw my first snow, a large patch just below the crest. The views were stunning in all directions but the Alps, which were supposed to be sometimes visible, could not be seen. I lay in a high meadow of tall grasses and wildflowers, ate lunch, and thought life was good.

After I wound steeply down past the blue waters of the Lac du Schiessrothried, I met the 'Man with the Gold Teeth'. He was elderly, wearing a jaunty white cap and stopped me with a friendly greeting. He asked me where I was heading and I made the mistake of telling him that I was about to look for a hotel in the village of Mittlach. He launched into a tirade against Mittlach: there was no hotel there and, even if there was it would be terrible. He spoke a mixture of French and German but the German gradually triumphed. I must go and stay in the hotel he was holidaying in – the food was fantastic, the beer heavenly, everything was wonderful. The village he was talking about appeared to be a long way away, so I showed him my map and asked him to point it out. *Nien, nein,* he shouted, grabbing my arm and spitting through his gold teeth. He dropped my map on the ground and scrawled some lines in the dust with his stick to indicate the direction. I began to think that I was dealing with a madman, so promised him that I would go and have a drink with him there later and hurried off.

The track shortly bifurcated, with one path leading to Mittlach and the other in the direction my 'friend' wanted me to go. I chose Mittlach. According to the guidebook, the village had been founded in the eighteenth century by Tyrolean woodcutters and when this pretty place appeared the first thing I saw was a hotel – an old-fashioned French one – the type that appealed to me. The staff were welcoming and my room was cool and comfortable. When I went for a drink, hoping that the 'Man' would not come to look for me, the bar was full of locals and appeared to be split between German and French speakers, although there was plenty of cross banter between them. Bilingualism seemingly flourished here. An excellent four-course dinner rounded off a splendid day.

8 July

This turned out to be a day more different than any for the past month. For a start it was cool, then it got colder until, when I climbed back onto the crest the thermometer outside a farm read 10°, a drop of 24° in two days. The track from the valley gave a stiff, unyieldingly steep climb of over 700m before I reached the edge of the escarpment once more. On top, the route led across open meadows with wide views but in the west low dark clouds were threatening. I got confused by the guidebook at a point where my large-scale map had finished and had to take a compass-bearing to get back on route. Thick mist suddenly descended and it got freezing cold. I put on waterproofs for the first time in weeks and plodded on, trying to see the little red stripes which were well separated. I could hardly see 5m in front of me when suddenly I spotted two figures huddled under a tree. They were two Dutch youngsters who were doing the GR5 in sections. I think they were relieved to see me because the dense mist was worrying in that featureless landscape.

We joined forces and trudged on until a large black shape loomed and revealed itself to be a *ferme-auberge* – a welcome feature of Vosges mountain walking where meals and lodging can be had. The farm building had a restaurant attached and when we went in it was packed with tourists sheltering from the change of weather. We had hot chocolate and cakes and then started out again. I had gone only a few hundred metres when I realised that I had left behind my silk scarf – a highly regarded neck wrap for cold winds and for relieving the pressure of rucksack straps on one chaffed shoulder. Telling the two to go on and that I would catch up, I hurried back to the farm, picked up the scarf and started again into the mist, which by now was even thicker. I kept thinking that I would catch up the youngsters but they never appeared through the blanket of cloud. I hoped they had not strayed from the route.

Walking on alone in that uncanny silence, although the path was easy and level, I suddenly felt weak and began to lurch from side to side. Everything went blank and I found myself sitting in the grass having, presumably, passed out for a split second. I sat there for a while wondering what had just happened to me. Was this a warning? It was fourteen days since my last rest day, so it was possible that I was just reaching exhaustion. The day's stage was planned to end at Grand Ballon but when the mist lifted and I saw the ski resort of Le Markstein ahead, I decided to stop and rest for a day. My resolve to walk continuously to the end of the Vosges was broken by this fright; a let down after the previous day's exhilaration.

Great meadows of yellow daisies and marigolds carpeted the slopes around the resort, softening the metal ski pylons and other messy junk which follows this activity up into beautiful mountains. I booked into one of the hotels for two nights and was given a room in the attic which had four beds packed into the small space. Winter was the time for exploitation of the masses, obviously. It was a strange, scruffy place and they charged me 30 francs extra for a key to the bathroom!

9 July

It rained heavily in the night and it seemed that I got my wish about the hot weather with a vengeance. The killer heat was gone and up here, on the crest, the temperature in the morning was only 12°. After a late and leisurely breakfast, I strolled out, carrying a book and my drawing pad in a plastic bag, heading for a seductive grass-covered ridge which promised a good view. It was quite cool on the top but I found a snug shelter in some rocks, facing the sun and with a tremendous panoramic view of rolling mountains and deep, forested valleys. To the north I could see the whole length of the Vosges which I had just traversed, while to the south the bald rounded cone of the Grand Ballon, the highest summit of the Vosges and my destination on the next stage, was clear and enticing.

I lay for a long time with the meadows dotted with wild-flowers around me; larks were singing high and swallows and

Vosges from Le Markstein

swifts were whizzing past my head. I was more relaxed about taking the day off but I could still not resist planning. All the way now, without a rest day, to Lac Léman or bust. This was the promise I made to myself and then I sat up to do a drawing of the fascinating undulations of hills with the fretwork of trees crawling up slopes and along ridges.

The day got colder and when I saw several parties on the path which wound down the slopes below me towards the GR5, I was itching to get on.

10 July

Le Markstein was perched up on the crest of the Vosges at 1,200m. The day's stage of 29km involved climbing the highest mountain in the range and then a long descent to the plain of Alsace. It was a bright sunny morning with a cool breeze and the path to the foot of the final cone of Grand Ballon was a treat. A gently descending sandy trail led through the meadows, always keeping high above a mountain road where the traffic wound around numerous bends, allowing no chance for drivers to look at the splendid scenery. I felt superior.

The climb up to the top of Grand Ballon was different: a rocky trail first spiralling, then straight up loose scree but I enjoy steep climbing when fit, breathing deeply and passing groups of breathless day-trippers along the way. When the path eased suddenly, the bare summit was there, crowned with one of those enormous stone monuments that the French put up in honour of their war dead. This one was to the Alpine regiment, the *Diables Bleus,* who fought to the death for this useless piece of stony ground in the Great War. I thought about the architecture of war memorials and how so many of them really glorify war; the French, for instance talked here about the

Crest of the Vosges

'sacrifice' of their young men and the inscription on their tombstones was *Mort pour France.*

I remembered the contrast presented by the Vietnam War Memorial in Washington DC where the design, by a young female architecture student, was a plain, undulating wall of polished stone, engraved with the names of the dead. It was impossible to walk the length of this wall, passing groups standing silently looking at names, without tears. The militarists and advocates of glory and nation, however, were outraged at the simplicity and insisted that a bronze sculpture be added, depicting a fallen soldier being carried by his heroic comrades – perpetuating the myths of glorious sacrifice.

A young German couple clad in black motorcycling leathers stood looking at the monument. Were their thoughts with the uncelebrated dead of their own country?

The trail for the remainder of that long day edged gradually down towards the distant plain. At one point in the forest, felling and subsequent erosion had wiped out the path and all waymarks on a steep slope. I had to make a detour across a dangerously loose mud slide with a sheer drop, before being able to swing down to a track, using tree branches as holds.

The beautiful town of Thann appeared on the plain below, sweltering in the evening sunshine, and after eight hours' walking I was glad to get to a hotel and sit down with a cold beer. Dinner was not so successful because it was pure Alsacienne cuisine – food for carnivores – a *choucroute,* which was a huge pile of sauerkraut with a thick slice of that disgusting indigestible bacon, plus two sausages – one long and soft, the other short and fat. I really hate this kind of food; even the names put me off, reminding me of the German *würste, schweinebraten, tafelspitz, hackepeter* – ugh! French names sound, at least, appetising.

11 July

The temperature in Thann when I arrived was 28°, not quite as suffocating as in Châtenois but it was necessary to sleep with the windows and shutters closed because of traffic noise. I had to wait until 9 a.m. for the tourist office to open because the high mountain refuge I was heading for was popular and might have been heavily booked. All day the route was unrelentingly up, but fortunately, although the sun was scorching, most of the trail was in shady forest and, as I got higher, the breeze was deliciously cool. The views were now more spectacular than ever: the purple plains of Alsace to the east and south, to the west the crest of the Vosges and the graceful Grand Ballon still dominant to the north.

The trail went over the Col du Hundsruecken and crossed the historic Route Joffre, used by French troops in the First World War to reinforce and supply the outpost at Thann. The route was named in honour of Marshal Joffre, the French commander whose main characteristic was said to be his imperturbability; not even huge casualties or military crises were allowed to interrupt his pattern of two hour lunches, long dinners and regular naps.

My destination for a lunch stop was the *ferme-auberge* at Belacker. The low buildings of dark weathered logs were set in a delightful alpine meadow and I went into the gloomy interior to see what they had to eat. There were only two offerings on the menu: a farm cheese and an item with a German name. I choose this, hoping that it was more substantial than just cheese. A big mistake! It turned out to be that revoltingly hard smoked bacon of the previous night, tasting like string and impossible to chew, much less to swallow. I ate the bread and drank a litre of mineral water, sitting outside in the dappled shade of gnarled ash trees and admiring the view.

The guidebook time up to the Col du Lac des Perches was given as 1 hour 25 minutes but I took far longer than this and arrived out on top, sweat streaming, to be asked by an anxious French couple to explain the map and tell them where they were. This had happened to me so often that I presumed that my weather-beaten appearance – sunburnt skin and faded clothes – made me look professional. It was good for my French at least.

A 30-minute detour from the col led through a dense forest to the Chaume du Rouge Gazon where there was a modern refuge-hotel. It was cool up here at 1,100m and pleasant enough to sit in the evening sunshine, looking out over the grassy meadows, named the 'Red Meadows' after the slaughter here in that terrible conflict of 1914–1918. The southern end of the long battlefront was now close and I reflected on the silent trenches and ramparts I had passed, remnants of a war that ended on the eleventh hour of the eleventh day of the eleventh month of 1918. It was a war which killed ten million men and wounded 21 million and according to the historian Leon Wolff, 'It had meant nothing, solved nothing and proved nothing'.

12 July

The morning dawned with another clear, deep blue sky and it was already hot by 9 a.m., despite the altitude. The Ballon d'Alsace was only a short distance away but the climb was steep and tough and took me over three hours. The trail was sensational, sometimes switchbacking and then snaking along the contours of a near vertical mountain face, with the narrow path literally cut out of the slope. The final climb to the summit was hell: sharp rocks, loose stones and heat! I was pouring sweat when I abruptly emerged onto the flat top into hordes of day-trippers who had strolled up a gentle path from the mountain road only ten minutes below. My disreputable appearance was a source of curiosity to the stylishly dressed French and I had to endure inquisitive stares all the way down to the road.

Tourist hotels, restaurants and souvenir shops lined the roadside and I sat for a while with an overpriced lemonade, served by a surly waiter. The indifferent staff and noise of traffic helped me to decide to move on without lunch. It was downhill most of the way and on a narrow path in the woods I met a large party of French soldiers on the way up. They were mainly young, possibly recruits, all sweating and obviously suffering under military packs. They were led by a hard-faced sergeant who looked tough and was twice their age. He was berating them and as I passed he looked at me and said something to them on the lines of 'Look at that old bastard, he is able to walk better than you lot, so get a move on!' Of course, it might have been 'Look at that old bastard, he's buggered.'

It was not a difficult walk but the afternoon got hotter and hotter. There was a welcome splashing sound and around a corner a little river of water flowed over a rock face into a hollowed-out log. I drank and drank and then stripped off all my clothes and stood under the fall, savouring the pleasure of the cold stream flowing over my body. Suddenly the town of Giromangy lay below and I was at the end of the Vosges. Just twelve days, plus one rest day, for the traverse of the range was not bad. I was satisfied that I was still on target and with only the Jura now to cover, I could safely anticipate a break at Lac Léman, and companionship again.

There was a pleasant-looking little hotel on the first street corner and I walked into the bar to book a room. A voice called out 'Hey, hello Irishman.' Sitting at a table were the young

French walkers, François and Cristophe, last seen at La Bonhomme a week earlier. They asked me to join them and introduced me to a third companion, Christophir, who had teamed up with them for the next stage of the Jura. We had dinner together and afterwards sat out late in the warm darkness, drinking an excellent Gewürztraminer and swapping stories in an increasingly incoherent mixture of English and French.

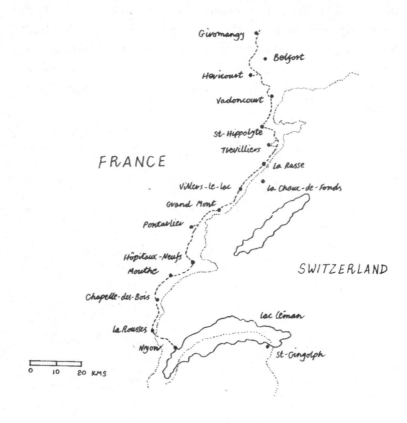

Map 8: Jura

CHAPTER 7

The Jura – Plateau and River Gorge

13 July

With the Vosges behind me, there were only thirteen days walking to Lac Léman. It seemed so little compared to the 64 days since I had left the North Sea. In that exultant mood I strode out from Giromangy to cross the flat expanse of the Belfort Gap – *Trouée de Belfort*. I walked fast on minor roads, despite the persistent and now muggy heat, as far as the great fort of Salbert. This was one of two Vauban-inspired forts on high positions guarding each side of the Gap. The GR5 led up to the 625m summit where a stunning view was promised. There was a perfectly simple and level path leading around the base of the hill but I decided to climb up to see the fort. I soon regretted this. The climb was cruelly steep on badly surfaced paths and the heat and humidity were now almost unbearable. To crown it all, I found the fort to be unimpressive; the view was non-existent owing to the thick heat haze.

In a bad temper and talking out loud to myself about what an idiot I was not to take the obviously pleasant lower trail, I barged down through the woods. Suddenly the N9 was across my path. I stood to watch the traffic speeding along and my memory went back 44 years to when I had cycled along this very route on my way to Rome. The city of Belfort was only a short distance away and I remembered clearly the Salvation Army hostel where I had asked for a bed. The guardian of the place was obviously concerned about the safety of the innocent student who had turned up on the doorstep of the shabby building and advised me to put my passport and money into my sleeping bag that night. I shared a malodorous dormitory with a score of rough-looking men, described by the guardian as vagrants, but nobody seemed to think that I had anything worth stealing. My other strong memory was of seeing rusty burnt-out tanks in the fields along the road – the detritus of the battle of the Belfort Gap in 1944.

There was an enticing restaurant across the road and I suddenly felt like celebrating or, to be honest, indulging myself with a typical French lunch. The Auberge Fleurie looked as if might be one of those marvellous, secret eateries which we are told can be found all over France. I had found precious few so far. The first encouraging sign was being warmly welcomed by a beautiful young woman, who was not put off by my scruffiness but tactfully showed me where to clean up before leading me to a table in the tiny dining room. The tablecloth was sparkling white and the wine glasses shone.

The meal lived up to my expectations and ended with one of the local speciality cheeses of the province of Franche-Comté which I had now entered – a soft delicacy called *La Cancoillotte*. As well as a litre of mineral water to kill my thirst, I had a bottle of delicious Alsace Pinot Blanc. I could have died and gone to paradise.

When I came out into the white glare of the early afternoon, I found it hard to get my bearings. There was a three-hour walk to lodgings and I did not think I would make it. I debated returning to the *auberge* and falling into bed, but the old resolve to push on regardless won out and I staggered down the road. Not long afterwards, on a deserted lane, I needed to relieve my overloaded bladder and turned to the ditch; it was then that I remembered the arrogant doctor on my 'retirement course'. One of his most patronising remarks was that, although age meant little change to health expectations, for the men at least the difference was that 'I can still pee over a ditch while you lot can only pee into it'. The trouble was that the bastard was right.

The memories of that afternoon are blurred but towards evening I came to a bridge over a huge autoroute, not marked on the map. It led towards Hericourt where I had reserved a bed. I wondered if the ordinary road had been extinguished, but a short distance over the bridge the old road appeared. My hotel was an old-fashioned one and the smiling man at the reception desk told me that he was new to the business and made me welcome. That night I enjoyed sitting outside a café watching French youngsters tossing firecrackers and bangers at each other in a pre-Bastille Day frenzy.

14 July

The giant key to my ancient room looked as if it might have come from the Bastille. The French National holiday dawned after a night of exploding fireworks and broken sleep. The friendly proprietor of this unpretentious establishment, where I appeared to be the only guest, was really welcoming for breakfast. Walking to Hericourt had involved a 3km detour from the GR5 and he told me that taxis would be impossible to find after last night's festivities; his wife would drive me back to the trail. My appreciation of the French rose even higher.

On the way back to the village of Brévilliers, Madame

asked about life in Ireland. She and her husband, having lived in big cities, now hugely enjoyed the French countryside. As we parted, she told me that a thunderstorm was forecast for later that day. I welcomed the thought as I trudged the village's deserted street, the ground strewn with the litter of the previous night's celebrations and the humid air thick with the smoke of burnt fireworks. I went badly wrong where a signpost had been uprooted and, frustratingly, had to retrace my route for 30 minutes to find the correct entrance to a forest. A long walk followed with distant thunder getting louder and the skies to the west darkening.

A spectacular storm of thunder and lightning, quickly followed by a deluge of rain, broke as I passed along the edge of a lake. Striding along in my waterproof, I enjoyed the cool wet, even though my shoes were filling with the water streaming down my bare legs. I crossed the big autoroute, the A36, by a footbridge and stopped to watch the rivers of traffic tearing along in clouds of spray. My way was along the bank of the Canal du Rhône au Rhin, a peaceful walk where I seemed to be the only person in the world. The route crossed this waterway at a lock but the passage was barred by a chained steel gate. I could clearly see the red and white waymark on the other side but a threatening sign proclaimed *Privé*. The lock-keeper's house was shuttered and two savage-looking dogs raged at me from behind the fence. There was no other obvious route, so I pushed my rucksack beyond the gate and climbed over, carefully avoiding the spikes.

The rain stopped but the humidity became worse as I arrived into the village of Vadoncourt in a lather of sweat. I booked in here to my first *gîte d'étape,* an amenity offered to travellers by many French villages in tourist areas where cheap basic accommodation is provided, often by the municipality. The quality of these varies enormously and this one was definitely at the lowest end of the scale. I was contemplating the crude bunks when a middle-aged Dutch couple breezed in. They were at the start of a few days walking towards the Jura and asked me to join them for dinner at a restaurant in the town which they could recommend from a previous visit. Joost and his wife Anne-Marie came from the Hague where he was a viola player with the Philharmonic. He was a man in love with life and his music. 'Why would I not be?' he said. 'I can get to play Mozart as often as I like.' His wife smiled and said, 'I get to clean the house.' We had an excellent meal: a Croûte Foriestière, a delicious dish of wild mushrooms, followed by carp, a regional delicacy.

15 July
This was the day when I reached the borders of Switzerland. Although I felt some sort of achievement, it was profoundly depressing to look at another map of France and see how far north I still was after over 1,300km. It was much cooler when I had started and I covered 16km fast and without a stop. I realised how much of my energy had been absorbed in dealing with the heat and, except for that sublime day on the crest of the Vosges, the previous weeks of walking had not been entirely enjoyable. At the top of a steep track in dense woods, I saw the first frontier stone which marked the border of the Jura province of Switzerland.

An old man was slowly coming down from the ridge of the divide. He asked me what route I was following. When I told him it was the GR5, he insisted on pointing to a path that I knew was wrong. He was really trying to help and, to humour him, I started out on the track he claimed was correct, meaning to swing off sharply back up to the ridge, which was the right direction. When I thought he was out of sight, I looked back and there he was, following me and shouting 'No, No, it's that way'. I thanked him and went on, hoping to outstrip him but the pantomime continued until I lost patience with my own forbearance and dashed around a corner, plunging up the slope out of his sight.

The trail led along the ridge and followed exactly the line of the frontier, which was marked every 100m or so with a neatly squared stone. These were carved on one side with the letter F and on the other with the figure of the Swiss bear; some of the older stones being elegantly engraved with the French royal fleur-de-lys and the date 1727. Near midday it had got hotter again and by the time I had reached the edge of the plateau above the gorge of the River Doubs, I was weary and limp with the heat.

I sat there for a rest. The panorama before me was now very different from any landscape so far on the journey. White limestone cliffs lined the river's deep ravine, sometimes rising directly from the water, and in places the steep slopes were thickly wooded. Up on the plateau on the far side were open fields and dark copses with the occasional church spire marking a village.

The village of Sainte-Hippolyte lay below on the riverbank and to reach it I had to negotiate a zigzag track down a near vertical slope. It was a picturesque place but with a distinctly run-down air. Hordes of tourists were in the narrow streets and macho French youths drove recklessly up and down blaring car horns. The hotel where I eventually got a bed was shabby, with indifferent service and the restaurant adjoining the bridge was no better. A flowery balcony over the river did not compensate for poor food and a couldn't-care-less attitude. Young waitresses were more interested in chatting up the male customers at the bar than serving food.

In the evening the terrace outside the hotel, however, offered the opportunity, as I sat with a glass of wine, of observing the promenaders. The crowds strolling around were mainly dressed in colourful shirts, shorts and sandals but two women dressed in sober beige outfits seemed different. 'I bet those are long-distance walkers,' I thought.

The Jura: on the way to St Hippolyte

16 July

My jaundiced mood lasted through breakfast and I left that noisy little place as soon as I could. Thick early morning mist filled the river valley as I crossed the bridge and followed a path through meadows of long grasses soaked in dew. To rejoin the GR5, I had to climb back up the north side of the gorge and then traverse under the cliffs, which by now were emerging from the cloud. The path crossed back over the river at the hamlet of Soulce-Cernay and began a long, agonisingly steep climb, through a gap in the white cliffs, up to the plateau. The day got hotter and the high sun was burning when I arrived on the flat top at the tiny village of Courtefontaine. I had to make a decision on the route here so I found a café with a solitary table outside in the shade. I studied the map to work out how to avoid a huge detour to locate lodgings for the coming night. The river took a big loop eastwards here and all the places to stay on the route, to where it rejoined the Doubs, were booked solid. The only village where a bed might be available was in Trevilliers, right in the middle of the plateau and a long way off the official trail. It seemed possible, however, to trace a way back to the proper route by linking up minor roads from Trevilliers without adding too much distance. The disadvantage would be that I would not have the comfort of the familiar waymarking to rely on but I was by now confident enough of my map reading to get me back on track.

A blistering 6km on roads followed. I had to watch out for daredevil drivers who wanted to squeal their tyres on every bend and was glad when the welcoming, flower-bedecked balconies of the Hôtel de France appeared. This establishment was a good example of the vagaries of French provincial hotel listings. It was not on a list but turned out to be an excellent choice and streets

Barn in the Jura

ahead of the miserable dump in Sainte-Hippolyte, which *was* in the official guide. The staff were welcoming, the room was pleasant and the place felt whole-some. The proprietor told me that it cost too much to get in the listing.

My meal that evening was wonderful, surpassed only by the inestimable lunch at the Auberge Fleurie: croûte foriestière, trout, baked ham with salad and five varieties of cheese; two of these were from the Franche-Comté region, *Le Comté* and the magnificently entitled *Le Mont d'Or ou Vacherin du Haut-Doubs.*

17 July
The village had a fête and the square was filled with carousels, dodgems and stalls filled with plastic toys and sickly-looking sweets, but the children loved it all and were wildly excited.

191

There was also a wedding celebration and dance and, all night long, processions of cars went through the streets. I had arranged for early breakfast, and a sleepy staff member was waiting for me with coffee and croissants at 6.30 a.m. He went back to bed after he had served me. 'Last night was rough,' he said.

The roads were quiet for a long time and, after the village of Damprichard, I climbed up to the Col de la Vierge where I had a magnificent view down towards the gorge of the Doubs. A narrow road, incredibly steep and with hairpin bends, brought me right back to the river and blissful shade. I rejoiced when I found the waymarks again. The route now led upstream along the riverbank and was a welcome change from the open country of recent weeks. The sound of the rushing water was delightful but soon a choice of routes was presented. The main path went back up to the lip of the gorge and descended to the water by the dramatically named *Échelles de la Mort* – the Ladders of Death. There was a variant trail continuing along the riverbank and I could see no reason for climbing back high except for the dubious thrill of descending the iron ladders. It had rained for an hour and the thought of stepping down metal ladder rungs with a heavy rucksack and wet shoes was not appealing. I continued along the river.

The gorge was dramatic; thickly wooded and only broken where vertical walls of white limestone rose out of the river up to the blue sky. The water was not attractive for swimming, and the notices warning of sudden flash floods from an electricity barrage upstream did not help to entice me. For some hours the far bank of the river was in Switzerland and when I rounded a bend in the stream after 27km of walking, I arrived at a little bridge on the frontier. The hotel here at La Rasse had been my goal for the night, but I was disappointed to be told that they were full – it being the weekend. The woman at the reception desk told me that the Swiss city of La Chaux-de-Fonds was quite close and there was a bus due in a few minutes on the other side of the bridge. Grabbing my pack, I dashed across to find two women with rucksacks waiting at the stop. I recognised them as the two I had guessed were long-distance walkers two evenings before.

The France/Switzerland frontier

We introduced ourselves on the bus. Yvonne Netenboom and Connie van Zanden were from Gravenzande, close to the Hook of Holland, and like all the Dutch I had met so far were walking the GR5 in stages. The bus took us right into the city centre and we went to look for a hotel. It was unsettling for me to be in a city again, my first since Nancy, but being Sunday the streets were quiet. We settled on a modest place in a side street and went out for a meal together, choosing an Italian pizzeria. After all the solitary evening meals, I found it hugely enjoyable to share a table with good company and not least to talk in my own language, the Dutch being so fluent in English. We swapped tales of the GR5. They told me that they had been walking the long distance trail now for three years, taking periods of two to four weeks, several times a year, and hoped to finish at Nice within five years from leaving the North Sea. They had planned to walk just two more days in the Jura and then travel to a Swiss alpine village where they had booked on a mountain training course to prepare themselves to cross the Alps the following year.

18 July

We shared a taxi back to the frontier bridge at La Rasse but there was an understanding that we would walk separately, the possibility of meeting again at the end of the day being left open. The arrangement suited me since I preferred to walk at my own pace and had well settled into my daily rhythm of solitary motion and musing.

Several hours of wonderful walking followed. The path clung closely to the swerves of the riverbank, but occasionally climbed steeply to avoid cliff barriers and down again to cross little flood plains of sand and tall grasses. At times the track was dangerous, with crumbly limestone shale on steep slopes where I had to clamber up by pulling on tree roots. One section was sensational where the narrow path was cut out of the vertical rock face. A flat platform followed with a dramatic view of the river valley and the artificial lake and dam called the Barrage du Chatelot. A series of steep metal ladders and staircases led to the dam with the deep gorge far below on one side, while on the other the placid expanse of the lake stretched away to the south.

The area was a national site called the Saut du Doubs and crowds of day-trippers, many of whom had come by boat, packed the lakeshore. There were hotels and restaurants and at one of the outside café terraces I met Yvonne and Connie again. According to the GR guidebook, it was possible to travel by boat up the lake to Villers-le-Lac, the end of our day's stage. The alternative was a boring 7km road walk. I then had one of my regular internal debates about the morality of straying off the official trail. Taking a shortcut where the GR5 wandered off to a local beauty spot and back again to more-or-less where it started from was easy to justify. Dammit, I was walking to Nice, not out for a day's stroll. After all, Patrick Leigh Fermor took lifts on canal barges, in cars and even travelled for weeks on horseback. Missing a lousy 7km road walk wasn't such a big deal. Then I remembered all those kilometres I had walked in the wrong direction; retracing my steps; the detours to find a bed for the night. It was time to withdraw a few kilometres from this huge deposit. I *would* take the bloody boat.

The two Dutch women had no qualms about the river trip and even the Sierra guide recommended taking the water route. It was bliss sitting out on deck, watching the wooded banks and rocky escarpments slide past until we disembarked right at the edge of the little town of Villers-le-Lac. The others had already booked a hotel and eventually I found a bed in a shabby but friendly place where I was solemnly guided through what they called my fire escape route, an incredibly messy barn. A useful hour was spent in the tourist office making future bookings. Yvonne and Connie joined me for dinner and we had an enjoyable evening, agreeing to journey together on the following day. Walking back to our hotels, I spotted the young Frenchmen, François and Cristophe, last seen in Giromangy. They told me that the third member of their party had gone back, but that they were determined to reach Mont Blanc.

I was secretly pleased that I had kept up with their pace for two weeks and felt that, with Lac Léman now only seven days ahead, I was definitely going to make it to the Mediterranean.

19 July
For the first time since early June in Belgium, it rained almost all day. I met my two Dutch companions after breakfast and

we set off to climb to the top of the forested ridge which marked the frontier with Switzerland. We caught up with the two French lads who were labouring under their huge rucksacks, now covered in oilskins, which made them look like round bundles with legs. I just got wet but the pleasure of not struggling along under a hot sun soon wore off and I began to feel cold as well as damp. Along the crest of the ridge we paused for a rest and François and Cristophe passed us and plodded on. I never saw them again.

When the ridge petered out into more open country, there was a frontier post and as the Swiss building, a few hundred metres east, seemed to have a restaurant attached, we trudged down to it to shelter. It was closed, from 2 to 26 July, for holidays. The rain was really pelting down when we arrived outside the picturesque Vieux Châteleu. Yvonne and Connie planned to end their walk here and I went with them to have coffee and a respite from the deluge. The place was booked out, so I had no option but to push on another 5km to my destination, Grand Mont. We made our farewells and promised to keep in touch with news of our success or otherwise on the long trail.

Almost immediately after I started out again into the now thick mist and rain, I went badly wrong. The poor visibility caused me to miss a tiny waymark noting an abrupt change of direction. It was only when I faced up to the dreaded situation that no red and white flashes had shown up for at least twenty minutes that I knew I was off course. Back through a dripping forest and across a meadow, I arrived at where I guessed I had made the mistake. The waymark appeared and to reach the proper path I had to negotiate an electric fence which was too high to step over. The only solution was to drop my rucksack across and then carefully crawl under the lowest strand.

The newly built *gîte* at Grand Mont was in a cluster of alpine-style chalets. When I arrived at the entrance, I was presented with a locked door and a notice stating that it would open at 5 p.m. It was now 3.45 and I was soaked through and very cold. Under a porch, I changed my wet T-shirt for a dry one and put on a fleece jacket, but when a hour and a half passed with no sign of life, I was beginning to shiver. There was nowhere else to go and I was miles from another village. I had noticed the window curtains in a chalet opposite twitching occasionally and eventually an old lady appeared and expressed concern about me. She brought me into her home and offered hot drinks and large slices of cake. I assured her and her elderly husband that I would survive and when a car drove up to the *gîte* at 6.00 I left, thanking them for their warm hospitality.

The owners of the *gîte* were very apologetic and a hot shower, change of clothes and a stiff drink mellowed me considerably. The building was built entirely of wood and was well equipped and spotless. There was only one other guest, a delightful young Swiss woman who was cycling through the Jura. We had dinner together, shared a bottle of red wine and talked about everything in a mixture of English and French. She worked with mentally handicapped children and played the cello and was the sort of young person who was full of life and a joy to be with.

20 July
The day dawned cold and damp with wreaths of mist floating over the dark, coniferous woods. I was high on the plateau at 1,034 metres and it felt like a place which could be unforgiving in really bad weather. My destination was the town of Pontlarier, 5km off the route, as the hotel on the GR in the village of La Cluse-et-Mijoux was full. It started to rain again soon after I

left Grand Mont and as I plodded down a slippery forest track, I took a heavy fall on a muddy section. I fell back on my rucksack but the only damage was to the pack and my rain gear which were plastered in sticky muck. The way forward at one point was extremely confusing. There were fallen trees everywhere and the only obvious route, according to my map, was clearly marked with a 'Don't go' sign. Eventually a red and white flash appeared and I followed it but after a few minutes I realised that it was leading in a totally wrong direction. I deduced that I was on a variant trail which could bring me onto a minor road leading directly to Pontlarier. Abandoning the attempt to find the correct GR in the chaos of fallen spruces, I set off on the variant up a steep hill to head directly for the road. A hellish nightmare of storm-damaged forest barred the track to the top of the slope and I had to fight my way over and under dozens of haphazardly fallen trunks until I could break out of the forest to a high pasture.

Thick woolly mist enveloped the landscape; the rain had stopped and the air was still. I had completely lost the waymarks but I guessed that the road was only about a kilometre ahead. The chances, however, of getting completely lost with this poor visibility were high, so I listened to hear any sound of traffic on the road. Everything was silent and I started off apprehensively across the open pastures on a compass bearing. A large cow suddenly looming out of the gloom gave me a fright and I then had to pass through a whole herd of beasts standing like statues and looking curiously at me. I almost stepped onto the tarmac surface before I saw the road and was mightily relieved.

Along the way I found a cattle trough with a water tap and tried to clean the mud off my back. I first washed the rucksack and then took off my shorts, which were wet anyway, and cleaned the thick coating off my rear end. Luckily no vehicle appeared because I'm sure I would have made a bizarre sight. The road walk was a lonely one, with the mist hiding all but a few metres on either side, and still no traffic appeared. It was as if the world had ended and, as I had reflected several times on this journey, it was a revelation to find such empty, peaceful places in the heart of Western Europe.

A few hours' march brought me into the large town of Pontlarier where I easily found a hotel. One of the straps of my pack was damaged and a search through the back streets revealed a shoe-repairer, who did a fine job of restitching.

21 July

The morning dawned bright and clear with a few wisps of cloud floating over the high, forested ridges above the town. It turned out to be an ideal day for a long walk – sunny but the air was cool, the temperature was below 20° and I walked fast and well, probably my most enjoyable day's march in nearly a month. The cheerful taxi driver who brought me back to the trail enthusiastically entered into the spirit of the hunt for the first waymark which would lead the way across the road. He spotted it first and triumphantly deposited me exactly where the route entered another forest.

The early stage was a punishing climb straight up to the fort of Joux, perched high on a mountain spur to command a narrow pass. The trail then went along the rocky ridge called Le Crossart; a superb walk with tremendous views. I met an elderly French couple going in the opposite direction who stopped and asked if I spoke French. I said 'Just a little' and they explained that they were lost and were looking for the GR5. There had not been a waymark for a while, so I directed them back the way I had come and they happily went off, thanking me warmly. Towards the end of the high ridge I had my first view of the great lake, Lac de Sainte Point, easily the biggest body of water I had seen since leaving the North Sea.

At Malbuisson I diverted a short distance down to this resort on the lakeshore to have coffee and a rest. The Hotel du Lac had a splendid terrace with colourful awnings and crowds of elegantly dressed French sitting at the tables. Marching onto the terrace, I threw down my rucksack and spread my dusty and sweaty self at a place in the sun. I think this was the first time since Lorraine that I had voluntarily sat anywhere but in the shade and I certainly looked out-of-place among the summer dresses, fashionable hats and white tennis clothes. Typically, the waiters treated me the same way as they treated everyone else at such a place – with disdain – and I waited half an hour to be served.

The last 8km of the day was over the mountains and through sub-alpine pastures to end in a valley at the ski resort of Hôpitaux-Neufs. A shapely mountain, Le Morond, rose above the town and the summit ridge was where a view of the Alps was possible. I was excited at the prospect, because this would be proof that I was in sight of my last barrier, albeit the most formidable of all, before the Mediterranean. One of the tourist shops had copies of the previous Sunday's newspapers – French, English, Swiss and Italian – and I enjoyed the long-denied, couch-potato pleasure of lounging at a café with *The Observer* spread on the table.

22 July

After 74 days of my journey and 1,500km covered since I had left the North Sea, I felt that the walk was now in every sense a way of life. Every day was different and yet in so many ways every day was the same. There was a rhythm about each day which was automatic. I got up about seven; packed my rucksack in the same order in less than five minutes, had breakfast and was on the trail by 8.30 a.m. The early part of the day usually involved a three-hour walk without stopping, then, if possible, a café rest and later lunch in the woods. The second half of the day was usually the most tiring but the hotel at journey's end enticed with a hot shower, a flop on the bed then dinner, ten pages of *The Forsyte Saga* and oblivion. It was the simplest of lives, where the only task was to find the way. My mood, however, could be different each day and of course there was a fresh landscape and new horizons facing me each morning, along the now interminable way.

The climb to the top of Le Morand was up a steep ski piste and near the top I had to traverse the slope and managed to give myself a nasty shock trying to cross an electric fence. After the summit the route went along the lip of an escarpment with a vertical drop over limestone cliffs on one side and gently sloped pastures on the other. At the *belvédère* on the corniche du Mont d'Or, described as dangerous in stormy weather, the promised view of the Alps failed for me yet again and all that I saw was a sea of cloud boiling up from the valley.

Several hours of pleasant rambling over wide pastures brought me to the little town of Mouthe as distant thunder was rumbling towards the south. Just before the finish, I passed the source of the Doubs, a waterway I had followed since Sainte-Hippolyte; sometimes on ridges above it or then along its banks, deep in the gorge. Mouthe has the unenviable reputation in winter of being the coldest place in Europe. It is sometimes called *La Petite Sibérie* and the temperature regularly falls to minus 30°, with a record low of minus 48° in 1888. On the plateau around the town the trees are stunted; on the streets the pavements are cracked, witness to the terrible frosts. Some of the high farms can be cut off for five months and I was told that the snow in places can be 5m to 6m deep.

23 July

A strange stillness and black skies to the south greeted me as I set out. Claps of thunder got gradually louder and lightning flashed over the woods in front of me. It soon started to pour as I entered a dark and wet forest and, although the paths were slippery, I made fast time to the pass at Le Lernier. The roadside here was strewn with cars parked on verges all the way up to the top of the pass, each with people sitting inside and obviously waiting for something to happen. I wondered if it could be the Tour de France because this was the time when the famous race took over the country. I waited for a while but there was no further activity and then pushed on up a sandy track where at the top I had a clear view of the road. I sat down to wait, since it had now stopped raining, but got fed up after twenty minutes and started again along a wooded ridge.

I could hear helicopters in the distance but the walk now was through pastures, little woods and along minor roads, with not a car or a person to be seen. The route was easy, and with the cool, almost cold day, I made really good time, eating up the distance to the end of the day's stage, the high plateau village of Chapelle-des-Bois. The houses were visible for a long way across the undulating fields and as I got nearer I could hear an amplified voice talking non-stop. When I arrived on the single street, there were hundreds of parked cars and crowds along the roadside. My hotel was right on the roadway and when I checked in, I asked, 'Is this the Tour?' and was told that 'Yes, and it is expected in fifteen minutes.' There was just time to order a beer and take up my position on the terrace before the roar of helicopters filled the air.

Within minutes a stream of traffic with police motorcycles and camera crews tore past, followed by a tightly packed mass of cyclists all travelling so fast and so close together that only one mistake could create a disaster. I was left with a lightning impression of multi-coloured vests, deeply tanned legs and taut, sweat-stained faces. The rearguard consisted of hundreds of vans, most with spare bicycles fixed on the roofs, and the whole circus was over in less than ten minutes. I felt a bit like Samuel Johnson, who when asked about his visit to the Giant's Causeway replied, 'It was worth seeing but not worth going to see.'

24 July

The pretty village of Chapelle-des-Bois sat at the base of a 300m wall of limestone cliffs and near vertical-timbered slopes, the crest of which marked the Swiss border. The main route of the GR5 tackled the wall directly to give a high walk along the crest, but for faint hearts and fragile lungs there was an alternative, gentler route which stole around the corner of the mountain ridge, avoiding the steepest climb. I chose the direct route, knowing I would revel in the demanding ascent. This turned out to be a cleverly engineered path with multiple zigzags, sometimes over polished pine roots and, more dangerously, across stretches of loose scree. Triumphantly I made the top and at the viewpoint called la Roche Bernard felt like the 'King of the Castle' as I absorbed a stupendous panorama of the Jura.

To the north, the way I had come, and to the west the geologic grain of the region was revealed: plateau, escarpment, precipice and plain; the Jurassic landscape where dinosaurs once roamed. To the south-west, wide pastures and dark patches of woods were interlaced with bright lakes. It felt good to be alive that morning and I was exultant that one more day would see me at Lac Léman, the lake of Geneva. I heard French voices nearby and four walkers appeared, two women and two men. We sat together for a while and they told me that they were doing a day-long walk on the GR5 towards les Rousses, also my destination. I enjoyed this human contact but decided to push on ahead of them.

The trail went straight along the crest past the boundary stones of the frontier and then into a great forest on a new plateau. The paths snaked through the trees with bewildering changes of direction but after an hour I became distinctly uneasy that I seemed to be heading generally south when my

Chapelle-des-Bois

guidebook map indicated a definite easterly direction. Trusting the *balisage,* the important rule that had served me well, I continued to follow the red and white stripes, but after just a kilometre was forced to admit that the route did not match the map. I was standing there reading the guidebook and wondering what the hell was wrong when the four French appeared. Consulting with them, I discovered that they had a new edition of the guide and the route here had been completely changed.

Abandoning the marked route in the guide, I strode off now with confidence in the waymarks and soon the trail turned on to the obvious line of the Crêt des Arêtes, the lip of a new escarpment. I seemed to be making very fast progress but made a stupid mistake when I was only about an hour from les Rousses. The red and white flashes were getting farther and farther apart until they disappeared and I was lost. The direction I was heading in was totally wrong, that much I knew, but where was I? Taking a compass bearing would not have brought me back to the correct trail but I instinctively pushed on uphill and suddenly recognised a spot, a peculiarly shaped tree, where I had been more that an hour before. I checked the map and saw that I had gone in a complete circle, the classic error in thick mist and equally easy in a dense forest. Guessing that the correct trail must have made a right turn somewhere ahead, which I had missed, I went on slowly and carefully, watching for a possible turn. At a rocky spur called Gros Crêtet I spotted a narrow path leading off the forest road and there was the waymark, half-hidden in the foliage. I had blithely continued along the road and contoured back the way I had come. Adding over 8km and two hours to an already long day exhausted me and nearly nine hours after I started, I arrived into the holiday resort of les Rousses.

25 July

A month of walking with only one rest day. As I started out I could hardly restrain my excitement that in a few hours I would see Lac Léman and perhaps the Alps. At Nyon I would also have covered two-thirds of the journey and have earned a rest. The long final leg of 27km started badly, however, when it became obvious that the older guidebook described a route which had been well and truly changed. I lost the waymarks at the huge Fort des Rousses but calculated that the GR5 must pass eventually through the frontier post at La Cure. The map showed a minor road leading towards the frontier and I followed it to where I hoped to pick up the trail again. The familiar red and white stripes appeared on cue to my great satisfaction but soon two directions beckoned. I deduced that one belonged to the GR9 or, as it is now labelled, the E4 – Pyrenees to Austria – while the other was mine.

The route took me past a large building at the edge of woods, where several coachloads of children were excitedly unloading cases and rucksacks. The French summer camp was another sign that the high season was upon me. The GR5 crossed into Switzerland at the town of La Cure, where, for the first time after numerous border crossings, I encountered frontier guards. They were stopping cars but ignored this disreputable pedestrian with the large pack, which could have been filled with contraband.

I was prepared to cope with the vagaries of the Swiss waymarking system which, as in Luxembourg, perversely and stubbornly ignored the internationally recognised red and white GR stripes and adopted a yellow lozenge or, where it suited them, a yellow stripe. Muttering to myself and sneering at this opting out by the Swiss, I quickly found the first yellow waymark and, after a kilometre, was pleasantly surprised at what turned out to be one of the best signed trails of the whole journey.

The splendid walk continued across a long stretch of pastures with herds of peaceful cattle and the sound of cowbells everywhere. A path gently descending by a shallow valley brought me to the main road at Saint-Cergue and the lip of the final escarpment above the lake. It was not yet visible through thick forests and the route kept close to the N90, a busy main road which came up from the plain in a series of multiple hairpin bends. The footpath went more or less straight down, cutting the zigs and zags of the modern road, following the historic Roman road into Gaul. The beautifully interlocked stones of the old road were visible in many places and it was a marvel that this ancient thoroughfare for the marching legions and their carts went straight up the hill while the modern traffic had to swoop endlessly back and forward to gain the summit.

Halfway down I came out of the forest and the vast lake levelled out before me. I looked for the Alps but there was only a shadowy outline of mountains visible in a blue haze. 'Foiled again,' I thought and wondered when I would get my first sight of Mont Blanc. The final stretch was in blazing heat across flat fields where the corn was ripening to yellow and then by a wide stretch of vines, the fruit now swelling out in bunches. The beautiful town of Nyon was laid out along the shores of Lac Léman and I walked down to where I could gaze out over the placid waters to the far side and contemplate my last stage – the grand traverse of the French Alps.

Map 9: North Alps

CHAPTER 8

Aiguilles and Glaciers –
Trek to Mont Blanc

10 August

When I stepped out into the early morning light, the red-gold spires of the Rochers de la Croix towered up before me. The first day of the traverse of the French Alps from Lac Léman began dramatically with the early sun igniting the tips of these rock peaks.

We three, Nuala, Nanno and I, had travelled up the short route from St Gingolph on the lake the evening before and, failing to find rooms in any hotel, had to settle for bunks in the squalid *gîte* in the village of Novel.

The period of two weeks since I had completed the long walk as far as Nyon was an intermission; peaceful but desultory and serving only to disconnect me from the journey. Three days early for the rendezvous back in Holland with Nuala, I went by train, first for a couple of days relaxing in Basel and then by the main line which ran along the banks of the Rhine. After reuniting in Nijmegen, we went to stay with Dutch friends on the German border but I realised that, while I had looked forward so much to meeting friends again, the re-entry into civilisation was difficult. Too many solitary days, a cosy and familiar routine that was unchanging and, most important of all, having responsibility only for myself made me feel uncomfortable in company and away from my beloved woods. Most of the time was spent reading, eating, swimming in lakes but always daydreaming of the weeks past. It was not long before I was itching to set off again and I suppose that the biggest problem for me was that the long walk was not yet over. Once Nanno was free to join us, we left one morning before dawn and, using the motorway network, arrived on the south side of Lac Léman in eight hours.

Climbing up into alpine pastures filled with wild flowers, we shook off the memories of the hovel where we had just spent the night: the unwashed blankets, the unspeakable toilet and, worst of all, the woman who had taken a bed in the communal dormitory while we were out to dinner and whose cacophonous snores went on all night. For me it felt wonderful to restart the journey. I was straining at the leash with the added pleasure of company to share the delights as well as the discomforts. The first stage up to the Col de Bise was a baptism of fire as an introduction to the real mountains. This involved a thousand metres of relentless climb and on the early part we were plagued with biting horseflies. These vanished as height was gained and, then, when we breasted the col, spread out before us was a spectacular view of the snowfields and glaciers of the beautiful Dent du Midi.

From almost 2,000m altitude, my highest point yet on the trek, the path now plunged down 500m to a deep green bowl surrounded by steep slopes. It was here that I had a severe foretaste of the problems to be faced in the remorseless ascents and descents of this long traverse of the Alps. Nuala and Nanno, who had found the ascent hard, now gaily rushed off down the slopes, leaving me far behind, carefully picking my

Alpine farmhouse

way down the multiple zigzags of the trail and aware all of the time of my vulnerable knees. Fifty years of climbing and a few injuries had left me with creaking arthritic joints which really hurt on any steep downhill sections.

On a 300m steep climb back up to another col, Pas de la Bosse, I caught up with them and we arrived together at the resort town of La Chapelle-d'Abondance after a hard, first-day walk of seven hours.

11 August

My feet had been giving me hell on the last stage of the previous day. The two weeks of rest had blunted the edge of my fitness and allowed my feet to soften again. The soles of my shoes had worn paper thin after 1,600km, so I supposed it was understandable that I would now feel every sharp stone. I had a fresh pair of special walking shoes for such an eventuality but since all my received wisdom about mountaineering was that boots were essential for the high hills, I decided to look for some now to wear for the rest of the trek. A ski shop provided a lightweight, inexpensive pair and I was glad to leave the scruffy old shoes behind in my hotel room, although they had served me well. There was added satisfaction in wondering at Madame's reaction when she found them because, on the night before she had scolded us for not taking off our footwear before entering her premises.

An overnight thunderstorm left the morning air cool, and under fresh blue skies we tackled the next climb up the slopes to the Col de Mattes. This involved yet another 1,000m ascent on a steep path, which at first wound up through dense scrub. We went wrong once and found ourselves floundering around in a thicket of willows where the path vanished. Finding the waymarks again, we came out into wide green meadows and lay down on the grass with the wildflowers of high summer all around us: lilac Alpine asters with their yellow seed pods; large white daisies; campanulas with their bell-like mauve flowers, and everywhere glossy yellow buttercups and delicate Alpine anemones.

At the top of the pass the views were stupendous but a cold wind drove us down the far side on an endlessly winding path to a rough track which led straight south. With two hours still to go, tiredness slowed our pace and when the skies blackened and the first rain turned into a downpour our spirits sank. We had to detour for 30 minutes down a tarmac road to a mountain refuge at Plaine Drance and we arrived soaked and exhausted.

We spread our wet clothes around a wood-burning stove in the centre of the communal dormitory and went upstairs to the dining room to drink beer and chat before dinner. We each admitted to being exhausted with these first days of Alpine ascents and descents and, after studying the maps agreed to a short next day. The dormitory was a primitive place which we had to share with ten lively young French who giggled for hours but they were very good-humoured.

12 August

It was a truly awful morning with cold rain and thick, swirling mist boiling up from the valley. We delayed as long as we could before setting out but were off before 8 a.m. into a very uninviting day. A 30-minute climb back up the tarmac road brought us up to the Col de Bassachaux where we stopped in dense cloud to find the way forward. We had an immediate problem as we searched but could find no waymark. The GR5 turned sharply here to cross the mountain divide into Switzerland and the guidebook maps were clear that the route now went off to the south-east. Visibility was down to 10m, so we had to take a compass bearing before setting out in the new direction. The rain ceased and the wind dropped and we walked in a strange stillness through the clammy fog and were mightily relieved when we picked up the first red and white paint flashes.

The path was level for a long distance and when it began to climb gently upwards, big gaps appeared in the cloud and we could see down into a deep valley with large patches of dirty snow on the north-facing slopes. The sky then opened up to a few flashes of sunshine but it grew even colder when we came up to the Col de Chésery and the Swiss frontier. The guidebook warned that the GR signs changed here again. Instead of the French white and red stripes, the Swiss had decided on a red stripe on a white square. I told the others about the perversity of the Luxembourgers and their waymarks; we decided that the Swiss did not want to be part of any international enterprise while the Luxembourgers were too rich to bother.

A coldly black Lac Vert lay at the foot of another pass and the path went around the rocky shore before climbing up to the Col des Portes de l'Iver which, at 2,157m, was another highest point for me so far on the trail. The view from the top was stunning, dominated as it was by the icily gleaming Dent du Midi and the great snow dome of the Grand Mont Ruan. The ski village of Les Crosets was far below and we debated whether or not to push on down to its more likely fleshpots after the bad experience of the previous night's flophouse. Halfway down the steep slopes of mainly rocks and scree there was another mountain refuge, Chaux Palins, and when we stopped for a rest on the terrace we decided that the extra walk down and back up again from the village was too much, so we booked into the place there and then. When we saw the dormitory, we regretted our decision. It was even worse than the one the previous night: a vast chilly loft with mattresses on the floor and one outside toilet with a cold water tap.

The short day, only three hours walking, and the long afternoon rest, however, were what we needed and we spent the time talking, reading, eating and drinking. There were only six others staying, and two of them, both women, a German and an Austrian, said they were walking the GR5 all the way to Nice, having started at Lac Léman. We had a typical fondue for dinner and the view out to the great peaks of the Swiss Alps in the evening light was sublime.

13 August

For some reason the woman in charge of the refuge was in a bad temper that morning, the coffee was cold, the breakfast was miserable and we were glad to see the back of the place. It was a chilly morning although the rain had passed, leaving the valleys lost in a sea of cloud but the mountaintops and ridges were clear and bright. Our early stage was a long climb up to the Col de Coux, only 100m above our night's refuge but, frustratingly, the route first descended 200m to avoid crags and steep, unstable, scree slopes. We made fast time, however, in the cool mountain air and reached the pass in well under the time given in the guidebook, always highly satisfying. Matching my time against the guidebook figure had long become an obsession on the journey, combined with all of the other calculations and estimations I kept making. At times on road walking sections, I was even prone to counting my steps. The

Near Samoëns in the French Alps

others, I imagined, thought that I had gone quietly crazy. Imagining, fantasising, cogitating, all went hand in hand with my solitary state. I was rapidly becoming a walking hermit. On top, we were back into France again and a fresh panorama opened to the west of green valleys and foothills. The trail again descended into the upper pastures of the Morzine valley and was followed by another steep climb to the Col de la Golése. The sun came out and we lay down on the grass for a long rest. This pass is an important passage for migratory birds and, according to our guidebook, ornithologists regularly check the numbers of birds passing through. The most celebrated migrators, it appears, were the black titmice on their way in the autumn to as far south as Eygpt. We hoped that the bird-watchers outnumbered the gun-mad French hunters.

It was a long, steep descent of over 900m to the town of Samoëns far below in the valley of the Giffre. The sky ahead was filled with paragliders floating along with the air currents. By the time we arrived at the lowest level, it was hot again and the change of temperature from the heights was remarkable. The hotel we found provided baths and, best of all, a swimming pool.

14 August

My feet had started to hurt again the previous day and the only explanation I could think of was that it must be the new boots. Walking so far and for so long had obviously conditioned my feet to every contour of the soft flexible shoes. Blisters were developing and my ankles were chaffed. Shortly after our start along the banks of the Giffre, I had to call a halt – I was in agony. There was only one solution: off with the boots and on with my spare pair of walking shoes. The boots I stuffed in my pack, to be used later on any snowfields I had to cross.

The Giffre is the largest tributary of the Arve, that great torrent fed by the glaciers of Mont Blanc. The fast-flowing stream was milky white from the suspended sands and gravels and to me the river was spectacularly fresh after the turgid, polluted waterways I had passed since leaving Holland. A metal footbridge led us across the racing waters and the route went straight up a steep rocky gorge where the vertical sections were overcome by steel ladders. We lost a considerable height again as the trail snaked down a pine-covered slope with polished roots ready to trip us. Open pastures followed with the ancient monastic centre of Sixt, founded in 1144, on the other side of the river.

A dramatic view, darkly backlit, of the massive Tête à l'Ane opened up in front and we had a clear sight of the pass, the Collet d'Anterne, towering above us. We would have to cross it before day's end. The waymarking suddenly vanished as we picked our way through clumps of alders and willows where the paths had been washed away by the mountain torrents. Crossing a lacework of rivulets and sandy flats, we decided to head for the Cascade du Rouget. The waterfall came over the cliffs in a misty spray and the flow spread over the black rocks at the base. Dozens of people gathered here as the fall adjoined a road and, like most beauty spots, attracted the inevitable café. We followed upwards to where the road ended with hundreds of cars parked everywhere, causing chaos as some tried to leave while others attempted to pass on the narrow mountain track. Another café stood here and we sat down to a light lunch, feeling superior as we watched the harassed motorists trying to park. A steep stony track led up to the upper cascades and we walked this section with hundreds of day-trippers, some tearing along, others straggling, but we marvelled at one tiny lad, no

Above the Giffre

more than six, who marched up with the measured gait of a seasoned climber. A future mountain guide, no doubt.

The main mass of tourists were left behind at the falls and the track now traversed across the steep screes and below the crags of the Pointe de Sales, following a dramatically elevated rocky shelf, until we emerged onto the grassy flat top of the pass. The Chalets d'Anterne appeared as a group of blackened timber huts across the alpine summer meadows and this was our destination after a hard six-hour walk. It was already crowded and we encountered the maddening French mountain refuge system of refusing to allocate bunks until 6 p.m. From experience we knew that the French always break the rule and sneak in to grab the best beds early. This time the guardian was strict and fair and everybody was allocated a place, one by one, just after the time.

The evening meal was the usual simple affair of a mountain refuge. Red wine by the flask made the crowded steamy common room bearable. The bunk rooms were in separate huts – primitive affairs with timber shelves and mattresses packed together. Ours was unfortunately shared with hysterical French teenagers who shouted and fought for hours before silence descended.

I had to go outside to find the toilet in the middle of the night and, emerging, was transfixed by the immense black sky above and the millions of stars sparkling with an intensity not seen anywhere except in high mountains or deserts. The Milky Way was a frosty crescent overhead and I tried to recognise some of the other constellations but could only guess at Orion, the son of the Roman god Jupiter, and was that Sirius – the dog star – glittering just below?

15 August

We left just after dawn and walked across the meadows past the still, black waters of a little lake to climb the easy grass slopes to the Col d'Anterne. Suddenly, as we neared the top, a startlingly white tip of mountaintop appeared, lit by the rising sun. Then, with every step upwards, the great snow dome, glaciers and icefields of Mont Blanc rose before us like the backdrop of some epic theatre, needing only a crescendo from Holst's *Planets* to complete the sensational drama. We were speechless at the spectacle.

Mont Blanc

For me, all the frustrations and disappointments of failure to see the mountain from the distant Vosges, again at Mont d'Or in the Jura and finally from the shores of Lac Léman were forgotten with the splendour of the great mountain filling our new horizon. It was a sublime alpine morning of intense blue sky and sunshine, flooding over the ridges and crests, now lighting the valleys. We still had a long hard walk down into a deep rocky gorge and another agonisingly long climb back up to surmount the final barrier, the crest of the Aiguilles Rouge. The roaring mountain torrent in the gorge was crossed by a temporary bridge and on the diagonal climb up to the final crest Nuala and Nanno paused for a rest while I rushed on, eager to look over the ridge and down into the valley where Chamonix, the Mecca of mountaineers, lay.

At the top of a shallow gully, filled with snow, I came onto the sharp crest where, across the deep dark valley, a stupendous panorama of peaks unfolded. The black pinnacles of the famous Aiguilles of Chamonix were directly in front; the sinister Dru with its perfect spire; the jagged edge of the Grand Charmoz (a mountain I had cause to remember) with the sharp tooth of its satellite stabbing the sky; Aiguille le Grepon; Aiguille de Blaitière; Aiguille du Plan, and the pure white summit of the Aiguille du Midi. On the right, everything was dominated by the huge mass of Mont Blanc. The great glaciers, the Glacier des Bossons and the Glacier de Taconnaz, sent frozen rivers of ice down to well below the tree line and higher up the shattered ice cliffs showed blue beneath the vast snowfields of the summit slopes. The final magnificent cone of the mountain was gleaming white against a perfect sky. I was overwhelmed by the sight but most of all by the memories of over 40 years before, when I was young and filled with passion for climbing those peaks.

The Aiguilles of Chamonix

Sitting there on a rocky outcrop, waiting for the others, I remembered. The graves of two of my climbing friends from the early days were in the valley below: Fred Maguire and André Kopczinski, both killed on the peaks opposite. Fred was a fellow student in Dublin, in the University College School of Architecture, and it was his talk about climbing, over our drawing boards in the sprawling studio, that first brought me to the sport in 1948. Fred was a rebel, a non-conformist and, in the repressive educational régime of the time, such stances were not tolerated. He was a brilliant draughtsman, but could become easily bored. One day as we were completing a sketch design project, Fred added a series of perfectly drawn black ink footprints to his drawing, as if a tiny figure had walked barefoot over the paper. The joke was not appreciated and Fred was given a reprimand and a 'fail' mark for his affront to authority.

On a summer morning in 1952 he had started out with his friend André up the early snow fields for a traverse of the Grepon and Grand Charmoz peaks when, for some inexplicable reason, he fell on an easy slope and slid down into a crevasse, dying of head injuries. Two years later André Kopczinski was killed when abseiling from the Col du Peigne, only a short distance from where his friend had fallen. André was a dynamic figure in Irish climbing groups in the years after the Second World War when, as a Polish veteran of that war, he was placed as a student in Dublin. He was handsome and charming and had a daredevil attitude which made him a brilliant climber. It was sad that a broken abseil sling would kill him when he had survived the war. In the terrible battle of Monte Casino in 1944, his job was to drive trucks across the plain under murderous barrages from the guns on the heights.

In the year after Fred Maguire was killed, I came to Chamonix. It was not my first climbing trip to the Alps, because in the previous year I had a good season on the easier climbs of the Austrian Tyrol. For some time I had partnered Frank Winder, a newly graduated scientist, on rock climbing exploration in Ireland and he and I travelled across France on Frank's beloved motorbike. Frank was one of the pioneers of rock climbing in Ireland and renowned for his new routes on previously unexplored crags. He had a passion for botany and was likely to cry out for joy on some hopelessly difficult rock passage about a rare plant he had spotted while I worried that he was about to plunge off the cliff. I was intimidated by the scale of the Chamonix peaks and the savage verticality of the rock faces but went along willingly when Frank and Peter Kenny, another pioneer of Irish climbing, decided to attempt the north-west ridge of the Grand Charmoz. This was a hard route which, only three years before, had its first ascent by two acclaimed French alpinists, Allain and Schatz. Along with another Irish climber, John Morrison, our party decided to team up with Harold Drasdo and Keith King, two English climbers known to Peter and Frank.

Our progress was painfully slow on the long rock pitches and it was late afternoon when the lead twosome arrived at what climbers call the crux, the most difficult section. This was just below the summit of the peak and involved fixing the rope up high and then swinging out across the vertical rock face in a hair-raising pendulum. After several attempts to get to this point it was nearly dark and we decided to retreat. I have horrible memories of trying to descend a steep gully in total darkness, using a top rope, before we all came to our senses and agreed that we must stay on the mountain in what climbers grandiloquently call a bivouac. There are planned bivouacs when alpinists have all the equipment to survive sitting it out up high but we had no such and our thin, army-surplus, cheap anoraks and woolly sweaters did nothing to keep out the numbing cold of that long night. At first light we moved off down to the snow slopes and saw a column of climbers far below and moving up. In our innocence we thought this must be a rescue party for us and resolved to ignore them or pretend that we had planned our night out. When we met them on the easy ground, we saw that they were army recruits and had no interest in us and later, on reaching the track, we lay down on the grass and slept in the warm sunshine.

Nuala and Nanno joined me on the ridge and we sat and talked about past mountain adventures but all the time I was aware of a deep sadness in myself, confronted with these majestic mountains. It was a confusing mix of a sense of loss for those friends who had died in the hills but, perhaps, more to do with my own lost youth and that those big mountain climbing days were over. I also had an acute awareness that I had survived, though only just.

My career as a serious alpinist ended at 8.15 on the morning of 19 July 1967. It was my first visit to Zermatt, which, along with Chamonix, are the two most famous places in the history of mountaineering. My companions were Peter Shortt, Pat Colleran and Frank Doherty, or Doc as we called him, and the climbing trip was intended as a training run for a forthcoming expedition to unclimbed peaks in Greenland. We had just completed an exhilarating traverse of the jagged arête of the Leiterspitz and now intended to climb a peak known as the Alphubel before attempting our main objective – the Matterhorn. The evening before, we had met two English climbers in the Täsch mountain hut at the base of the climb. Dick Hale was an ebullient young charmer, acting as a professional guide to earn money to keep him in the Alps throughout the summer, and was there with his client, Eddie, who was inexperienced.

We had started well before dawn so as to complete the ascent ahead of the rising sun warming the frozen loose stones on the rock faces. The early part of the climb was up a long but fairly easy section and there was a forewarning of trouble when a few small rocks whizzed past, dislodged by the English pair, who had started ahead of us. I advised our party to pick a line up the face to keep us clear of this hazard, always a possibility with a clumsy climber, and the rest of the route up to the final rock tower went without incident. This section began with a narrow steep gully and I was acutely aware of the danger of being in this with other climbers directly above: a gully being a perfect chute for dislodged rocks. We resolved to climb it as quickly as possible and move out of the firing line onto the open face of the tower. Peter and Pat went up fast and climbed away from the potential menace, and Doc quickly followed them to a safe place. Then it was my turn.

It happened then. There were frenzied shouts and a great black mass of rock came thundering down on me. A terrible blow tore me from my holds, the world turned upside down and I was falling clear with the rocks. The rope jerked tight – oh God – Doc had held me! I spun around in the gully, my right hand burned into the rope and my left leg was turned around, smashed and held by the muscles. It was essential for me to get out of the fall line and I frantically scrambled to one side as more, smaller, rocks smashed into me. I could now hear the others screaming up at Eddie, who had started the fall, to stay still. Seeing a small overhang, I crouched under it and coiled a spare length of rope around a spike to relieve the weight on Doc. The small stones were still coming and rattling off my helmet and when I knew I was safe for the moment, I gave way to waves of pain. They will never get me out of here, I thought, and I didn't think I could stand the torment much longer. I tried to pull my leg, with the boot turned the opposite way, up to a foothold to ease the agony.

The others shouted down to ask how I was and I was able to tell them that I was safe for the moment. Dick and Pat decided to go for help and climbed to the summit before taking the easy route down across snowfields and the glacier. Peter climbed down to me, on a top rope held by Doc above, and first tried to splint my leg with his ice axe but it was impossible in the constricted position and I couldn't stand the pain of manipulating the limb. We were on a face which was still in the shadow and frozen but it would not be long before the sun moved round and then the whole area could be swept by falling stones, loosened by the sun's heat. It was imperative that they move me to a place which would be out of danger of stonefall to wait for rescue. There was a suitable small ledge jutting out of the face a short distance away and Peter now tried to manoeuvre me there. I put my arms around his neck while he faced the slope and slowly moved off. It was the worst experience of my life. My smashed leg kept tangling up and Peter was exhausted with my weight. He cut a few handholds in tongues of ice and, with me pulling on the holds and him lifting me, we finally got to the ledge – a sort of platform high above the glacier.

Doc then brought Eddie, not injured in any way, down to join us in the safe place and they tried to make me as comfortable as possible. Shock descended on me then in great shuddering spasms. They adjusted my leg to stretch it out despite my howls of agony; the femur was smashed in several places but when they covered me in a special metal foil blanket – a newly invented piece of emergency equipment which I was carrying – I settled down and the shock waves died away. I was more frightened of my back where the rock, as big as a table, had grazed me, tearing my ice axe from my straps. There was a terrible burning pain which I endured until I got the courage to reach around behind me for the source. A sharp piece of metal bolt, used for belays, was digging deep into me and when I shifted it, the relief that my spine was not broken almost brought me back to normal.

Hours passed with no sign of rescue; black clouds over Monte Rosa growing bigger all the time worried me but the others tactfully didn't mention the possibility of a storm. Then Peter shouted, 'Look at the light flashing below.' They lifted my head and there, on the lower glacier, I could see what they thought was the red light of a helicopter. Hope came flooding back and I felt that I would live. Days later, in the hospital, they told me that the 'light of hope' was the Swiss flag flapping in the breeze beside the refuge.

Eight hours passed and now the others were silent. What had happened to Dick and Pat? My mind was far away and I was in a sort of delirium when somebody shouted, 'There it is!' The helicopter suddenly rose up in front and its clattering roar enveloped us. It hung there a few metres from the face while from the open cabin helmeted figures looked out. There was no chance of getting a line to us from that position since the face was too steep. The machine descended to the shoulder of snow below the rock face and two men jumped out. When they rapidly climbed up to us, we saw that one was Dick; the other was a local climbing guide. Dick's first concern was to do a proper splinting job on my shattered limb, since I had to be immobilised. He used three ice axes and long lengths of nylon climbing rope looped around me and in the process stopped the guide from tying an unsuitable knot in the sling which was to connect me to the helicopter line.

In the meantime a rope was being rigged across the gully and up to a larger platform which jutted out of the face. They lifted me onto this ropeway and clipped me in position and then, with me hauling hand over hand and others pulling, I rose slowly along the line. Near the top the rope jammed and I was howling with pain but then a sharp pull got me on to the platform. The helicopter roared in but quickly swooped away and I heard the guide muttering that it was too dangerous because the rotors could crash into the face. This happened again and again and I felt black despair. The others were not discouraged and hauled me out to the very lip of the platform and waited for the machine to come back. In it came again and I saw the rope line sailing towards us, and then it was grabbed by frantic fingers and clipped into my waist line.

There was a ferocious jerk, a howl of engines and I was snatched right off the mountain – out into a void. I had a last glimpse of the figures standing on the platform and then saw the glacier far below my sailing legs. It all happened so fast that I had no time to check if the clip to my waist loop was closed properly. I closed my eyes and desperately gripped the rope above the link until I knew I could not support my weight any longer and gradually loosened my hold. Nothing happened and, opening my eyes, I looked up at the helicopter and saw the co-pilot leaning out. He grinned and waved and I knew that I was on my way back to life.

It was like a dream, suspended from a slender line and floating over dark ridges and white snowfields until green meadows and trees appeared below and I was lowered to the ground outside the refuge. The helicopter landed and I was lifted into the cabin for the last stage to the roof of a clinic in the village of Zermatt.

The darkness was like a black pit. Pain enveloped me but worst of all was a raging thirst. I was lying on my back and couldn't move my legs: they felt bound, as if in a vice. I called out but everything was silent. Delirious now with fear and pain, I didn't know where I was or what was wrong. As I fumbled around for a light switch, memories came back: being lifted from the helicopter and trundled into a building; an elderly doctor telling me I must have an operation and then – nothing. Finding no switch, I panicked. Shouting for help and thrashing about, I slid out of the bed onto the floor and everything faded.

I opened my eyes to a room flooded with daylight and

several people around me. My left leg was suspended from an elaborate system of pulleys and wires and the burning pain had returned. The elderly doctor chided me: 'You try to get out of bed and now your operation no good. We have to do it again.' A nurse gave me a drink and then some painkillers and I drifted back to oblivion.

Hours later, I think it was, I came back to near normality and realised all that had happened. Glad now to be alive, I didn't dwell on the iniquity of being left alone in a dark room after a serious operation. This was, after all, my first experience of being hospitalised. Drowsy with the painkillers, I began to feel a sense of elation and arranged for a telephone to talk to Nuala and tell her I was all right. She had already got the news and said she would come out to Zermatt as soon as she could. I drifted in and out of sleep and lost all sense of time. One memory stands out and that was on the following day when the two helicopter pilots appeared looking for money. When I had been lifted into the machine at the refuge, the first words they said to me were 'sign this', putting a piece of paper into my hand. They had now come to collect. My wallet had been delivered to my room by my friends and I emptied it to pay them off.

Nuala arrived and seeing her unloosed a flood of emotions in me. Lying on the mountain ledge, I tortured myself that I could be leaving her with three young children to raise and that my folly would cause such pain. Maybe this well-inherited Catholic guilt helped me to survive. The doctor arrived and announced that he would operate again next morning and that it would be better for Nuala to go for a walk in the woods. The implication was plain – I might not recover.

I have no memory of that second operation. Afterwards I was told that a long, stainless steel pin was driven down from below my hip to tie all the bits of shattered bone. It didn't bear thinking about. My other injuries were minor – a damaged right knee cap and cracked shoulder – but I was now resigned to a long immobilisation. I did not know then that it would be nearly three years before I would walk again without crutches or stick.

A steady succession of climbers, Irish and English, came to see me and, although they could not help it, their tales of climbs past and to come depressed me deeply. My window looked out to great snow slopes above the village and beyond to the shining ice pyramid of the Breithorn. Every morning I could see files of climbers ascend the path which led up to the glaciers and I wondered if I would ever again walk the hills.

I spent six weeks at that hospital, which my friends told me was actually a hotel. Seemingly, if the guests injured themselves skiing or climbing, then their room was changed into a hospital room at greatly increased cost. It was run on a shoestring and maybe that was why I got tetanus. One morning I awoke in agony and, in a near delirious state, felt my jaws clamped tight. Nuala described the doctor, who owned the place, standing over me saying 'Vy you not open your mouth?' Lockjaw prevented any retort, much less the one I wanted to give the unfeeling bastard. The treatment was nearly worse than the condition: massive painful injections over several days. It dawned on me afterwards that the attendant who took me down for my operation was also in charge of the horses which the hotel used to transport visitors from the railway station – the village being car free. Zermatt also had a typhoid outbreak some years before. I wanted to get home before this place killed me.

Eventually the doctor told me I could leave and that he would put me in a plaster cast which would soon allow me to walk on crutches. He then presented me with a huge bill which included a hefty amount for treating the tetanus which I had contracted in his establishment. I told him I could not afford to pay all at once and that a portion would have to wait until I got back. He accepted with bad grace and Nuala, who had faithfully stayed with me all this time, made arrangements for me to fly back from Zurich.

The journey home went smoothly. Swiss efficiency was at least evident in planning the various rail journeys to the airport, with porters taking charge of my stretcher at each connection. I had to lie flat on the floor of the trains and my last memory of Switzerland was the bad smell of Swiss feet.

When I arrived home, my own doctor took one look at me and sent me to an orthopaedic hospital. The consultant surgeon did not say much but ordered that I be admitted at once and put into a new cast which I thought was modelled on a straitjacket. My left leg was totally encased from the ankle while the right leg was left free below the knee but the worst was the body encasement right up to my upper chest. I had to lie flat on my back, on a solid mattress with only my head and neck free to move. The early days of this were torture and I did not think I could bear it, but in time I got used to it. A warm September led into a colder October and it was not until near Christmas that I was freed from my armour and began tentative attempts to walk with crutches. I was given the impression, in the old-fashioned but kindly Cappagh Hospital, that they did not think much of the Swiss treatment. Someone suggested that flashy expensive surgery could more easily go wrong and conventional long-term immobilisation was more certain of success.

The year following my release from Cappagh was one of the worst years of my life. I was able to walk on crutches with my left leg clamped straight in a steel brace but all attempts to walk unaided failed. Several times a week I had physiotherapy and in these sessions, when I tried to walk a few steps without crutch or brace, my 'good' leg, as I always called it, left a wet footprint. My physiotherapist said that this was from the sweat of my effort to prevent any weight on the 'bad'. Everybody was puzzled as to why, when I was obviously fighting so hard, no mending was taking place.

Of all the depressing memories of that black year, one stands out. One summer afternoon, while dragging my braced leg along a city pavement, I was greeted by a friend from past mountain days. My replies to concerned questions about how I was getting on were pitched in that automatic, optimistic note I had resolutely fixed on since leaving hospital. We parted and I can still see the look on her face as she wished me luck. My feeling was one of abandonment. Being banished from the company of those with two good legs who could stride along high moorland or plunge down cascading scree slopes led me close to despair that awful year.

On a dreary November morning, almost exactly a year after I had left hospital and eighteen months after my accident, I had an appointment with my surgeon. His opinion was that the broken ends of the bones in my femur were not uniting but instead were rotating around the steel pin, causing the surfaces to polish instead of knitting. He said I had two options, apart from staying as I was – in constant pain. The first was to have a bone graft. This would involve taking slivers of healthy bone from my hip and placing these around the polished surfaces of the breaks. The bad news was that this involved a complete reprise of the first hospitalisations; a serious operation; months of entombment in another full-body plaster cast and a further six months or more of exercises. I asked what the second option was and he replied that it could be an amputation. 'If I have the bone graft what are the chances of success? I asked. 'Possibly 80 per cent.'

I was managing again to drive my car at that stage, having had the seat pushed back fully so that my straight clamped leg could depress the clutch. I drove out alone to a deserted sea front and watched the steel grey waves wash up the cold sands. As I stared over the wintry bay I felt all of the fears and disappointments of the past months; all the let-downs after high hopes and my old optimism was fading to nothing. I went back to hospital the next day.

The new operation was, seemingly, long and difficult. I knew nothing of it but this time when I awoke a strong feeling, best described as exultation, engulfed me. I knew my leg was healing! This was despite the fact that I was back in a mummy-like cast which held me rigid from upper chest to toe. Doctors and nurses, when I told them, smiled indulgently but I never felt more certain that I would now walk again. Three more months were spent on a hard bed but my optimism surged daily. I had a small drawing board rigged up to my bedstead so that I could resume my detailed designs for a new church, interrupted by my accident. Reconnecting to the world of work gave me a fierce sense of purpose and by the spring of the following year I was released.

Before I left the hospital, I had one of the regular visits from the resident doctor on his rounds. This time it was not my own surgeon but another consultant nicknamed, for obvious reasons, 'God'. Few of the patients in that place ever questioned the lofty medical hierarchy but I asked him if I would be able to go back to hillwalking or even mountaineering. His reply was a definite 'No'. 'In fact,' he went on, 'you will have to wear a special built-up shoe and rely on a walking stick for the rest of your life.' After he swept out of the ward with his retinue scuttling after him, I said to myself, 'Sod you, I'll prove you wrong.'

A glorious new spring for me led into the second summer after the accident and each week my leg got stronger. I embarked on a programme of walking up a hill each week. The summits got higher and higher and I was soon off two crutches, then the steel caliper went and finally I was onto one walking stick. After six months of exercise and physiotherapy, the last prop was thrown away. My antics in Zermatt, falling out of bed when my leg was in traction, left my 'bad' limb a little shorter than the other. After a brief but irritating experiment with rubber inserts in one shoe, I felt confident enough to throw these away too. Although the exercise régime was rigorous and constant, I never did regain full free movement of my left knee joint and my walking gait was, at times, a little uneven. On the third summer following the accident, the stainless steel pin was removed and after the operation the souvenir of my Swiss misadventure was left beside my bed. I was free.

I went back to Zermatt six years after that fateful July morning. Was it to exorcise those ghosts or was I trying to prove something? One memory of that return visit stands out. We were camping on a high moraine below the majestic Weisshorn and I saw spring flowers push up from under the melting tongue of the glacier. I knew then that I was happy just to be in the mountains. Later, standing on top of the icy Breithorn, I looked back down the valley and imagined I could see that clinic window.

It was time to move on. I wanted to revisit Chamonix after all those years and Nuala and Nanno agreed that we would go down to spend the night there. First we had to climb to the summit of the Brevent at 2,526m: the last section of this was a rock scramble using fixed wire ropes. On top the view of Mont Blanc was overwhelming but the *téléphérique* station and crowds of people were less than enchanting.

Nuala and Nanno on the Brevent

The long trip down by cable car was a pleasure, however, with shining snowfields, glaciers, rock spires, green alpine pastures and dark forests in a moving vertical panorama. Paragliders hung over the abyss, their multi-coloured canopies like exotic butterflies.

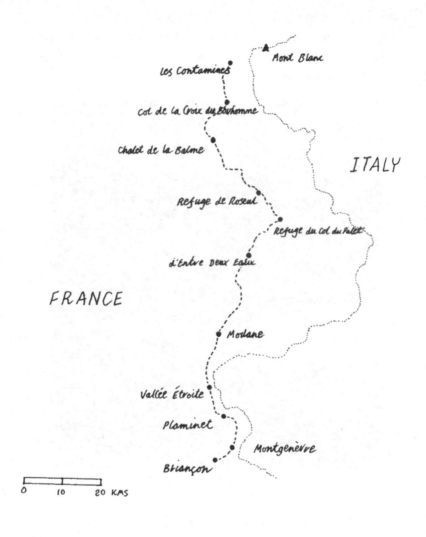

Map 10: Middle Alps

CHAPTER 9

High in Savoie – Peaks and Passes

16 August

After the 'highs' of the previous day, when we felt like gods, Chamonix was a huge let-down. We wandered this tawdry tourist trap, gloomily aware that we were part of the disease which has cheapened the justly famous alpine village, with its proud history of classic mountaineering. The narrow streets were filled with aimlessly moving crowds, mixed with slow-moving cars, and there was no feeling of excitement at the splendid peaks rearing up on both sides of the deep valley. The fixation appeared to be on the endless display of shops, each filled with alpine versions of visitor trash: nastily varnished walking sticks, all knobs and ribbons; toy ice axes, arrestingly chromed; ridiculous felt hats; edelweiss-decorated mugs; mountain panoramas in inlaid wood veneers, burnished metals or coloured wool; stuffed miniature chamois and mountain sheep, all packed together with the usual T-shirts and postcards. We bought cards and that evening, in a restaurant, we wrote to numerous friends, many glasses of wine dulling the memory of the indifferent meal. The recollection of the hotel we eventually found was of surly staff, cheap plywood furniture and crashing bottles and metal bins in the kitchen yard at 5 a.m.

It was a distinctly cool morning as we left the town and walked up the valley to regain the GR. The early sun lit up the tips of the peaks and high snows, but the deep valley itself was still cold and dark. We passed by the low-level cliffs of Les Gallands, where years ago we used to rock climb on days when the clouds closed in on the peaks: they were now used by a climbing school where you must pay for the privilege. Capitalism had come to the mountains.

The valley soon opened and we were in sunshine again, with the wide blue sky above. Our route was the low-level variant which ran along the banks of the Arve, a roaring white flood of melted snow and ice from the glaciers. A pleasant woodland stroll ended when we were forced sharply upwards by the deep scour of a recent avalanche. We crossed this high up along a mere scrape in the loose scree slope and held our breaths until firm ground appeared. A rough track then led steeply downwards, before the shock of Les Houches ski town and the problem of negotiating the crossing of a complicated road junction over the motorway to the Mont Blanc tunnel.

The thunder of the stream of huge trucks entering and exiting the 12km tunnel, connecting Chamonix with Courmayeur in Italy, soon died away and we sought a quiet terrace to map-read. Looming above us was the Col de Voza, and this was where we would intersect the main route of the GR5. A two-hour climb up to the pass involved criss-crossing a huge ski slope; the alternative was taking the direct *téléphérique*. The others were quite amused when I wrestled with my conscience about whether or not this was cheating. They thought it even funnier when I launched into a convoluted argument that, because the horizontal distances of the low and the high routes were the same, this justified taking a mechanical lift down and another one back up again. So we took the *téléphérique*.

On the far side of the col it was hot, the alpine sun scorching our heads and necks. The track down was steep and broken and my feet and knees began to suffer again. I found this deeply depressing; after so long on the trail, I should have been hard and fit. The truth was that my upper body was fit enough, but the continuous pounding on stony paths was taking its toll on my legs. My spirits were also low because Nuala and Nanno would be returning the next day and I would walk alone again for another three weeks.

At the village of Bionnassay we sat in the shade for cool drinks under the great glacier of the same name and with the Dôme de Goûter soaring above. When we came out onto the road which led to Contamines, there was a hotel directly opposite. An argument developed about whether we should stop there or push on up the hill to the town centre. I was for continuing on: my long-established obsession with achieving set distances inclined me to stop at the top of a hill rather than the bottom. The others thought this was ridiculous but resentfully followed me up the road. After we found a place to stay, the party was reduced to silence and it was long after dinner before either of the two would speak to me. My misery was complete.

17 August

Amity had been restored over breakfast and we made our farewells. Nuala and I arranged to meet at Nice on 11 September when she and our friend Cathie would fly out to welcome me. There had been thunderstorms all night and it was still pouring rain in the morning when Nuala and Nanno set out to walk back to Chamonix. I resolved to take a rest day: the weather was one factor in this decision but I was worried also about my painful knees. At the start of the journey I had packed a walking stick – one of the newfangled collapsible ski pole types. Being an old-fashioned mountain climber, I had scorned the need to use such an aid for actual hillwalking: my rationale for taking it was as a defence against aggressive dogs. But no canine attacked me and the stick stayed in my rucksack until Nuala asked to use it. She found it a great aid on steep slopes and it dawned on me that this could at least partially solve my knee problems. The trouble was that she had taken the stick with her. That afternoon when the rain eased, I bought myself a new one.

It rained on and off all day with intermittent thunder and lightning. I stayed in my room resting and reading from the final volume of *The Forsyte Saga,* which Nuala had brought out. The sojourn put me back into a positive frame of mind and I looked forward to tackling the steep climb up to the Col de la Croix du Bonhomme the next day.

18 August

Heavy mist filled the valley but the rain and the thunder had stopped. It was cold after the storm but ragged gaps in the clouds soon showed blue sky and an easy walk up the banks of a river gradually eased my sore feet. After the little chapel of Nôtre-Dame-de-la-Gorge, the route went steeply up, following a Roman road called Rochassets, which in sections was cut through solid rock.

At the Refuge de la Balme, the GR5 was joined by the famous TMB. This superb mountain walking route, the Tour Mont Blanc, undulates all around the great massif but is notorious for the huge numbers of walkers it attracts. The worst result of this was overcrowding of the mountain huts and refuges. I was not looking forward to meeting these crowds and sharing one night with them at the next refuge at the Col de la Croix du Bonhomme.

The promised hordes appeared on cue. For me, so inured to solitude, it was a rude shock. On one section of a broad track it felt like walking along a city street but as I climbed higher, the crowds began to thin. On a tiny plateau, the Plan des Dames, there was a large mound where, according to legend, an English lady and her maid had perished in a storm and they are buried on the spot. Every traveller was expected to place a stone on the mound to avoid bad luck.

The wind on the exposed heights felt freezing and I hurried on to the first pass, the Col du Bonhomme. I tried to shelter here under a large boulder and eat something, but the penetrating cold drove me on. Racing low clouds hid the view and stinging sleet met me as I came up onto the Col de la Croix du Bonhomme, at 2,483m, my highest point so far on the GR5.

The refuge was just below, a ten-minute scramble on a stony slope. It was quite a surprise. I was expecting a small, ramshackle hut and dreading the sheltering packed masses, but here was an obviously newly built, beautiful wood structure where I was welcomed by a friendly guardian. The first floor dining hall had windows on three sides and it felt warm and comfortable. In contrast to the usual authoritarian six o'clock allocation of beds, the guardian immediately showed me to a pleasant little room with four bunks which I was to share with an amiable Italian couple.

For the evening meal I was directed to one large table where the others seated were mainly French. A Parisian couple who had lived in California and who spoke English, along with their friend, a mountain rescue guide who had only French, were my immediate fellow diners. The lively exchange of stories in French and English lifted my spirits after a day when I was missing Nuala and Nanno.

In my room, I found that the fourth bunk was now occupied by a young Frenchman who was sitting up studying a long computer printout. He had the almost gaunt look of a serious athlete and this was confirmed when I asked him what he was doing. He told me that he too was following the GR5 from Lac Léman. I asked when he had started and he stunned me by saying, 'The day before yesterday.' 'How is that possible?' I asked, 'I have taken eight days.' He told me that he was trying to break the record of running the GR5 from Lac Léman to Nice in eight to ten days. He hoped to run 60km a day, carrying hardly any pack. He drank from mountain streams and ate only at the evening stop. It sounded like lunacy but since both my sons, Eoin and Colm, also indulged in this crazy, leg-breaking sport of hill running, I understood. He had a fascinating and shocking statistic, however. His computer printout was a rise and fall profile of the route from Lac Léman and the sum total of the jagged peaks and valleys was 27,600m. This was more than three times the height of Everest from sea level. Do I have to do this, I asked myself? It didn't seem possible since I was taking 30 days or so. Eight to ten days would be a tremendous feat, but only for a fanatic.

19 August

I had no sooner left the refuge than the crowds were gone. The TMB went off steeply downhill to the east while my way went south along the dramatically toothed Crête des Gittes. This was a glorious walk, swooping from one side to the other of the knife-edge ridge, but occasionally treading the very crenellations. I lost a huge amount of height coming down to the Col de la Sauce, but my elation died when I looked up at the towering slopes ahead of me.

The sun was hotter than any day so far and, even though I was deeply tanned I could feel every bit of bare flesh burning. The next five hours or so were a nightmare because the way forward was up a long, unrelenting slope, wide and exposed to the sun's glare. I vaguely remembered the torrent and waterfalls of Treicoll, but the guidebook mentioned that the trail went past the ruins of Chalet de Presset. This never seemed to come and I began to despair. I think that I then hit what marathon runners call the wall. When the crest of a pass unexpectedly appeared, I collapsed. While I lay there exhausted, I realised that I had misread the guidebook and had long since passed the landmark of the ruined building and was over the worst, on top of the Col de Bresson.

After a while I began to appreciate my situation. Surrounded by savage, jagged peaks, the pass was dominated by the superb pinnacle of La Pierra Menta rearing up to the south, while on the far side of the col a gentle slope led down by the fast-flowing Ormente. I recovered enough to walk on, but very slowly, which was just as well since the way down was incredibly rocky: a moon-surface, covered with rounded boulders. The low buildings of the little Refuge de la Balme appeared after an hour when I was near collapse again. There was a family of French walkers staying and I had to make an effort to talk to them at the evening meal.

Falling into bed at 8.30, I shivered violently before falling asleep, despite covering myself with a pile of blankets. I knew then that I was suffering from heat stroke.

I went out in the night to the primitive toilet and the whole rocky valley was lit by a dazzling full moon.

20 August
The previous night I had seriously considered giving up. I really felt bad and questioned for the first time why I was doing this to myself. Did it matter, I asked, if I abandoned the walk and took buses on to Nice? Who would care? When I thought about it the next morning, I saw that I had walked for eight-and-half hours and climbed nearly 2,000m, mostly in hot sun. No wonder I was exhausted and demoralised.

As had happened so often before, a new dawn saw me fresh and renewed. The valley was in shadow; the alpine air felt like wine and the path wound alongside rivulets, through grassy pastures and along sandy moraines, speckled with tiny wild flowers. In the damp fertile places there were masses of yellow buttercups and marsh-marigolds, while the meadows were dotted with blue-mauve campanulas. Where the river-banks were torn by winter flood waters, purple foxgloves thrived.

I walked strongly in the early bright morning, my morale restored. As the path dropped further down the valley, it got hot again and there was now more than a hint of the south about it: dry grasses with crickets chirring, down to the banks of the Isère river. After four hours' fast walking I decided to give myself a break and in the village of Landry a good French lunch felt like a splendid idea. It wasn't. The dining room filled up shortly after I had ordered, mostly with families whose children ran about the tables. The boisterous offspring were not the problem, however; it was rather the mothers who harangued and scolded them in loud, harsh accents. The meal was unremarkable and I felt that I would have been far more rested with bread and cheese on the trail.

The last section of the day's stage was up a steep slope which fortunately was in the deep shade of deciduous trees, mostly beech. The route zigzagged bewilderingly through the woods and I lost the markers time and again but since the route regularly cut across the switchbacks of a roadway, navigation was fairly easy. At the top of the slope the valley flattened out and the trail was along the banks of the Ponturin, now a torrent of roaring water. There were signs of colossal mud slides everywhere, probably after the thunderstorms of the past few days. At one point the bridge was washed away; this made crossing the fast-flowing waters tricky, even though the river was shallow. As I neared the refuge, another huge slide had closed the road and bulldozers were clearing a way through.

The Refuge de Roseul was a civilised place. It was beside the road and obviously attracted the car-borne masses, but fortunately they were mainly using the restaurant. After the previous night's primitive hut, it was a pleasure to enjoy a hot shower and a comfortable bed. The evening meal was good and I shared a table with the French family of the previous night who had arrived close behind me.

21 August

For a change I slept late and had a lazy breakfast. The prospect of a short day was a luxury to be savoured, although I knew that I would be just as tired after a short walk as after an epic trek. This was another inexorable rule of the long journey.

The mountain valley was serenely beautiful. The prospects were wide, with walls of snow mountains, dominated by the mass of the La Grande Casse, at 3,855m, the highest mountain

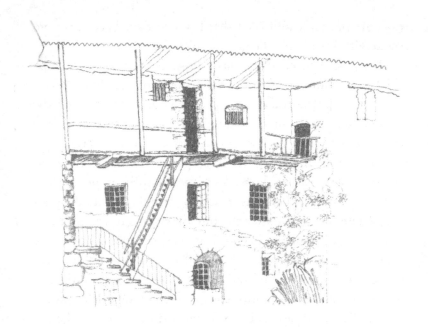

Farmhouse in Savoie

of the Vanoise. White cataracts flowed down the slopes on either side of the trail, which was up an easy slope, occasionally flattening out to meadows filled with wild flowers and where marmots popped out to peer. It was a paradise.

I was now entering the National Park of the Vanoise – the first such reserve in France, being set up in 1963 specifically to preserve the ibex. The Italians were way ahead of the French in recognising the necessity to save this rare species of alpine goat. The Italian government had created a refuge for the animal in 1922 in the National Park of Gran Paradiso, just across the frontier from the Vanoise. The invasive ski industry, however, now threatens the whole region.

The first signs of autumn appeared on the way up from the valley of the Isère. The rowan trees were in full fruit, with scarlet berries already heavy on the branches and distant groves of deciduous trees streaked with brown and russet. I felt it hard to believe that I had been walking all through a summer – from early May – and it would soon be September.

The Refuge du Col de Palet, perched on a rocky knoll, was a cheerful sight when I arrived about midday. The tables and benches outside on a rough gravel terrace were crowded with climbers and walkers and it was a huge relief to throw off my rucksack and join the early diners. Afterwards I found a sheltered grassy patch away from the refuge and lay down to snooze in the afternoon sun.

I had a decision to make at this point. There were options to the GR5 over the next few days. The main route went down to Tignes and the Val d'Isère, where it followed a low-level itinerary as far as the Arc river. There was a high-level alternative, the GR55, which cut right through the mountains. I drowsily contemplated these choices on my high resting place and came down in favour of the *haute montagne* route. One advantage of taking this track was that it would save a day; I felt that I needed this to be sure to reach Nice on the appointed date. The best argument for this course was, however, that the low-level route passed through a mess of ski resorts, some of the largest in the Alps.

The French family, parents and three boys, were again at this refuge and we greeted each other as old friends. They planned to climb a nearby small peak on the next day and invited me to join them. I was tempted, but my ingrained obsession with getting on made me reluctantly decline.

22 August

Leaving the refuge, I climbed to the top of the col in fifteen minutes. Compared to the unspoiled valley I had just traversed, the new view was a brutal contrast. Way below lay the ski town of Tignes and all the slopes beneath the col were dotted with pylons and wires while the flanks of the mountains were scarred and slashed with wide tracks for ski runs. Vegetation fought a losing battle against erosion and raw earth patches blotched the miserable scene.

Walking across this landscape, or rather wirescape, was a depressing experience and I had to go down closer to the town to find the path up the far slope, away from the desecration. The architecture of Tignes was typical of developer design everywhere: hotels and apartment blocks of identical units piled on boring pile, all in styles which defied category. The concrete cliffs and repetitious cubes were oblivious to the magnificent architecture of the mountains: the pyramids of peaks, the enduring buttresses of rock, the whole symphony of ravines, scree slopes, fractured ice precipices and serene snowfields.

My new path led me steeply up into a superb, hidden valley. I looked back once, when I had breasted the last slope and was rewarded by an unexpected last view of Mont Blanc. The upper snows and glaciers sparkled in the midday sun and the mountain mass filled the northern horizon. Turning away, I faced due south and the prospect now was the great tumble of lower peaks which had to be traversed before the Mediterranean. I had never felt better than when I swung along an easy track: clouds of tiny pale-blue butterflies swarmed around my feet and here and there the ground was starred with the electric-blue of alpine gentians. There were several snowfields to be crossed, but the careful placing of my trek stick kept me from slipping on the hard-frozen surface. At one stage I had to cross a torrent almost buried in deep snow drifts. The snowbridge looked reassuringly thick, but it was still nerve-racking to look down at the raging waters through a deep hole in the snow.

I heard a whisper on the wind and looked up to the upper snowfields of the Grande Motte, which towered above me to the west. There, in the tiny dots flowing down the white slope, was a reminder of the ski industry invasion: summer skiers whose shouts were faintly carried on the breeze.

This was a solitary walk and one of the best days I have ever had in the mountains. A little lake tempted me to have my first swim since the Ardennes but it was a shock to plunge naked into the glacial waters. Lying on a sun-warmed rock afterwards was pure pleasure and I would have liked this journey to go on for ever.

At the Pont de Croé-Vie, a substantial wooden bridge which spanned the torrent, I had to leave the GR55 and go east to join another high-level variant of the GR5. I had been seven hours on the trail and it was time to stop. The assemblage of traditional alpine farms which made up the Refuge d'Entre-Deux-Eaux was snuggly tucked into the gap between two valleys and I arrived none too soon to secure a bed. The place was crowded and even more so when a large party of Italians arrived, complete with a train of mules to carry their gear.

23 August

How I hate crowded huts. I was lucky, I suppose, to get a bottom bunk in a small room, but alpine huts where nobody opens a window and where there is invariably a thunderous snorer are not ideal for restful sleeping. I slept badly that night and lay awake for hours wanting to strangle one cougher and snorer.

I left early, anxious about the long day ahead. Losing height to the crossing of the Termignon was frustrating and a further annoyance was that there was not a single red-and-white marker to point out the start of the GR5. A signpost indicated the way to the Refuge l'Arpont, however, and I knew that this was on my route. Striking out up a steep slope, I became aware that the weather was changing. Ominously liver-coloured clouds filled the sky and the first mutter of thunder began long before I had reached the easier slopes below the Glacier du Pelve. When the first rain arrived, I seriously debated abandoning the high-level route and retreating to the valley tracks before it was too late. I kept walking, still uncertain about the best course of action while the rain now pelted down and thunder crashed overhead; fortunately there was little lightning. Several rivulets had been stepped over and when I came to a bigger flow, which had become an uncrossable brown flood, I knew that there was no return: the earlier streams would now be similar torrents.

There was no way forward and no way back. I remembered an identical dilemma posed when I was climbing with Nuala in the Austrian Alps a few years before.

We were traversing a steep slope, having crossed a high pass, and were heading for a bridge, marked on the map as the only crossing of a deep river gorge. When we reached the river, we found the remains of the timbers that had been washed away. Cliffs barred the possibility of descending directly, so we decided to climb higher along the edge of the river until we could cross in safety. We were forced higher and higher until the slope eased out almost under the glacier. The river here was split into several channels and it appeared to be a good deal shallower and with a less violent flow. Experience had made me wary of alpine torrents and so I positioned Nuala upstream to anchor me as I attempted a roped crossing at a broad section. The first channels went easily, but when I stepped into the final stream I was immediately swept off my feet, even though the water was only thigh deep. Nuala held me on the tightened rope and I grabbed a boulder on the far bank. I had been pulled under the water by the fierce power of the glacier flow and emerged drenched. We repeated the process with me anchoring myself upstream while Nuala had the same experience which, for both of us, left us shivering as much from sheer fright as the wetting. Without a rope, one or both of us might have been dead.

I had no rope and no companion. The slope up was loose scree, but not very steep, so I set out to climb higher and hope for a bridge which should have been there on a well-known route. I was almost at the tip of the glacier when, through the driving downpour and ragged mist I saw a timber construction. It was just a few planks resting on rough stone piers and it was almost awash with the flood. I doubted that it would last very long in this storm, so I raced across. How many more of these, I wondered? It was a savage place up there on the frontal moraine, with great white cascades everywhere. The whole world seemed to be under water.

There were still no paint markers but there was a faint trace of a trail in the stones. Pressing on, I crossed over innumerable smaller streams but none as ferocious as the one behind. The Refuge d'Arpont appeared out of the mist and I gratefully sheltered there for an hour until the worst of the storm passed. The remainder of the trail was a grinding plod where I just put my head down and after one of my longest days reached the town of Modane.

24 August

How do some hotels in France survive? This was my thought when I realised that I was the only guest in a main street establishment. It looked as if late August was past the end of the summer season. My room was comfortable and quiet with a view up to one of the tremendous forts built when Italy ruled the region.

After the gruelling experience of the previous day, I slept late and the sun was well up when I started. Almost at once I was faced with a cruelly steep uphill haul: under the motorway viaduct into the Fréjus tunnel. The path was at an impossible gradient – scored straight down through the forest – and I concluded that it was actually a steep downhill ski run. It was also, unbelievably, the official route of the GR5 and again I cursed the ski industry for its spoliation of the beautiful mountains. Despite the toughness of the climb, I found that I was going well and came over the top of the slope, into the village of Charmaix, in well under the time given in the guidebook. Along the way there were many reminders of the wars over frontiers which had plagued the Continent for centuries. Ruined strongpoints and other military installations dated back to the Franco-Italian wars of the nineteenth century.

The landscape was dramatic, dominated by the bare rock of boulder screes, precipices and jagged peaks while the lower slopes held stands of larch, now yellowing for fast-approaching autumn. The Col de la Vallée Etroite was easily gained and the view this time was a long way south. Ridge after ridge of pale-blue mountains faded into the far distance and I began to imagine that one day soon there would be a break in the rolling high country, revealing the ocean.

The valley walk down was easy and, although it had been

a long day, over seven hours, I felt strong and reflected that morale was the most important element: my body's response to the task each day depended entirely on my attitude. The previous day I had been exhausted and my nervous strain during the storm was more than responsible.

A roadhead appeared near the valley's end and the Refuge de la Vallée Etroite was perched beside it. The mountain hostelry was owned by the Italian Alpine Club and for some hours on the way down from the col, I heard more and more Italian spoken by the increasing number of walkers I met. I was warmly welcomed and had a four-bed-room to myself. For dinner, the amiable women guardians put me at a small table of French speakers because the main body of guests was Italian. I could join in the polite conversation of the French, but the Italians in the dining room, mostly men, were in high good spirits, the wine flowed, and the songs and jokes were uproarious, if incomprehensible. The meal was superb, putting to shame the generally uninspiring food I had endured in France. I enjoyed the evening and the Italian wine and my closeness to the borders of Italy felt like real progress.

25 August

I was sorry to leave, reflecting that this was one of the best mountain refuges I had ever stayed in. Several cups of splendid *café au lait* sent me off in high spirits with the prospect of a short, easy day ahead. The route led up behind the refuge towards the Col des Thures and, while the early slope was nearly vertical, the crafting of the path was masterly. It was carved out of the steep slope, snaking in a barely perceptible gradient across the face of the near cliff, then looping back and forth in dramatic hairpins, offering different views at every turn. It was a hillwalker's dream track, gaining height effortlessly.

It was almost an anti-climax to find the slope easing into a broad ramp leading up to the pass. I met crowds of walkers on this section and was puzzled as to where they had come from because I had met nobody on the narrow track up from the valley. There was a tiny placid lake just below the Col des Thures and when I breasted the rise, a new vista opened below. I had climbed from the refuge fast and, since I had the whole day to walk 16km, flopped down below a grassy knoll to contemplate the view. Most of the other walkers had the same idea and it was agreeable to sit there listening to the murmur of voices and occasional laughter from the scattered groups.

Wide alpine pastures lay below the col and the walking was easy. Tight flocks of sheep flowed across the grassy uplands and I made rapid speed down to the ruined Chalets des Thures. The crowds had vanished and it appeared that most of the walkers had climbed up to the col and then returned to the valley roadhead. The trail arrived abruptly at a sharp cliff face and the way down into a semi-circular coomb was by multiple zigzags through a forest of pines. Huge erosion had torn the steep faces into strips of raw red earth, and formations of yellow rock pinnacles gave the place a fantastically alien look. Lower down the woods were silent, the air was full of the scent of resin and the track carpeted thickly in fallen pine needles.

The village of Chapelle des Âmes was on the valley floor, on the banks of the fast-flowing Clarée and the French guidebook described the traditional pastoral way of life in the valley of the river Clarée. Unfortunately the ski scourge has arrived in this backwater, as in so many other parts of the Alps. New apartment blocks, hotels, pizzerias and souvenir shops were already rising while the steel pylons of ski tows crawled up the slopes.

I crossed the torrential Clarée by a footbridge and walked through a forest of stone pines, across an alluvial plain towards my night's stop at Plampinet. A tiny sunlit clearing beckoned off the trail and, because I had plenty of time, I diverted to this for a lunch stop. The air was resinous with the sap of the trees and the floor of the clearing was a deep mat of sun-dried moss and lichens. I dozed here throughout the afternoon and left the glade reluctantly when the sun dipped below the trees.

High in Savoie: near Plampinet

Plampinet was a pretty and as yet unspoiled village of traditional alpine buildings. There was a tiny sixteenth-century church, complete with wooden furniture of the same period. An old *auberge* offered a bed and I had a somewhat primitive room with a window above the roaring river. It was a relaxing place and I enjoyed making a drawing of the traditional houses and barns. The restaurant where I ate that evening was a different story and notable only for the worst meal of my entire walk. An elderly French couple at the adjoining table left most of theirs: a fatty bacon without any flavour, served with a glued-together tangle of pasta and a spoonful of doubtful vegetables. It was awful. The couple called the waiter, who was also the proprietor, and made some mild complaint. He gave

Plampinet

an exaggerated Gallic shrug and stalked off, leaving the couple staring in disbelief. The previous night's Italian feast was a fond memory as I drank more of the rough local wine.

26 August
Another beautifully crafted path, with long switchbacks, led up from the village and I made short work of the climb. The day was cold, particularly in the deep shadow of the gorge, but wonderful for hard mountain-walking. Past a hamlet of clustered wood chalets a superb hidden valley, the Vallon de l'Opon, opened up. This provided a splendid walk and I strode along at a fast pace, thinking now that six- or seven-hour days are no problem to me, whereas earlier I could think only about how long and hard each day was going to be. The mountain scenery was dramatic above the tree line. I was tired of forests and the prospect of open grassy meadows, guarded by the scree slopes and bare rocks of the Pointe de Pece, was a tonic to my already high spirits.

The 1,000m climb to the Col de Dormillouse seemed like an afternoon stroll and I confidently pushed up the last steep rise to gaze at another intoxicating panorama. A great mountain amphitheatre faced west where a narrow gap in the rock wall of the Crête des Pece formed a natural proscenium. Through this gap the jagged peaks of the Dauphiné seemed startlingly close in the clear atmosphere. Nuala and I had walked around this marvellous Ecrins National Park eight years before, on a superb GR called the Tour de l'Oisons. The passes on the sharp lip of this high bowl reminded me of the innumerable high cols, some knife-edged, which we had crossed on that earlier trip.

An enticing track contoured across the concave slope and then ascended to the far lip and the Col de la Lauze, another knife edge with a new panorama away to the south. On the far side a quartet of climbers was just coming up the last few steps to the col and I greeted them when they arrived. They were two Dutch couples who were in great good humour when they reached the summit. They were all of a good age and one told me he was 80. They were walking the GR5 in the reverse direction every year, taking three weeks at a time, and hoped, they told me, to reach Holland before any of them died. I congratulated them and sped off down the new slope feeling young and frisky.

A good way down a green valley I stopped for lunch under the shade of a grove of gnarled larches and fell asleep for an hour. Afterwards, I hurried down through woods to where, on a little cliff edge, I was almost on the frontier with Italy. A few minutes to the west was the ski resort of Montgenèvre where I found a room in a small *gîte*. This was run by an English couple who relied mainly on the winter sports season but who assured me that they also wanted to cater for summer walkers. I was again the only guest and John and Judy could not have made me more welcome. It felt good to drink cold beers in the comfortable lounge and also to be able to speak English freely. An excellent meal was shared with them, the wine flowed, and they told me that two Americans were three days ahead of me, going all the way to Nice.

27 August

It was another beautiful morning, with an intense blue sky and warm sun but with a distinctly cool air, hinting that autumn was creeping in. I left the Gîte le Cairn, concluding that it was one of the best lodgings I had experienced on the journey.

The walk down from Montgenèvre to Briançon was under three hours and I stopped in the woods along the trail for a rest.

I had a swelling in my left ankle which had been growing for some days and which I had been trying to ignore but now it began to worry me. It was quite painful to touch but so far it did not affect my walking. My optimism of the day before about easily finishing the journey was jolted and I hoped the pain would not develop. Reckoning that I had fifteen days before my rendezvous in Nice, I calculated that this would involve eleven days of hard walking, leaving me with four days to spare to rest my ankle. I hoped it would not be necessary but resolved to stop at Briançon to see if the swelling would go down.

I arrived into this high-altitude city at midday and crossed over the elegant 1754 stone bridge into the old town. This was another of Vauban's dramatic fortified places, with great stone ramparts dominating the older houses and narrow streets with their fast-flowing gutters in the centre of the walkways.

The new town was spread out below the ramparts and I walked down to find a hotel. I went out later to a pharmacy to get some advice about my ankle but the counsel from a helpful pharmacist was predictable, if not what I wanted to hear. 'What should I do?' I asked. 'Stop walking' was his answer. Continuous pounding for 2,000km had done its damage, but I had to go on. He gave me a pomade as an anti-inflammatory ointment and an elastic bandage. I hoped it would work: the ankle was now very sore. A hot, humid afternoon in the lower town deepened my gloomy mood.

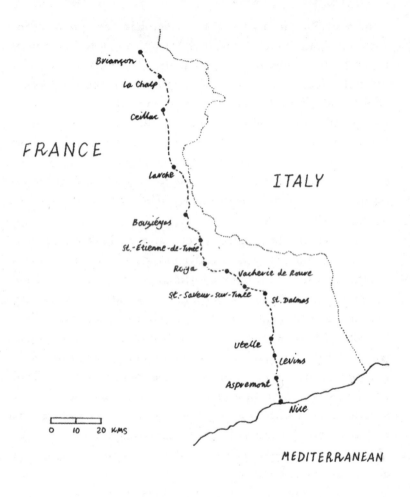

Map 11: South Alps

CHAPTER 10

Alpes Maritimes – Into the Warm South

28 August

The cool morning and clear blue sky put me in good humour and I faced the long, 1,200m ascent to the Col des Ayes enthusiastically. After the first steep climb by a deep gorge, I reached the hamlet of des Ayes. There is still a local population living there, in traditional houses which were typical of high mountains: thick walls and tiny windows. The day warmed up considerably when I got out of the shadow of the gorge; there was nobody about and at one rivulet I sat for a while devouring deliciously sweet wild raspberries. There were, however, many signs now that summer was nearly over: the grass yellowing and foliage turning russet and gold. Leaving Briançon, I saw a large group of youngsters, very subdued, loading their rucksacks and camping gear into coaches. Schooldays are starting soon and it seemed strange to me that I began my trek long before the schools closed for summer camps. The French were going home, but I was still walking.

My ankle began to hurt again and I inspected it to find the swelling was getting worse. Over the top of the col I stopped at a spring and bathed my foot in the clear cold water. I had a long rest but the condition of my ankle was now really worrying me. I thought that a sensible course would be to take a longer break from walking and hope that the swelling would go down. Resolving to stay for two days at the next night's stop, La Chalp, I moved off slowly down to the next valley.

Just before the village there was a large pond ringed by trees and I had a swim in waters a good deal warmer than the glacier-fed lakes of the high mountains. Even with this restful break, I arrived in La Chalp tired and despondent. The *gîte* was full, so I booked into the only hotel to discover later that, because of a fête, the restaurant was closed. The only food I could get was to gatecrash a festival barbecue which the locals were having, after a series of grass-toboggan races.

29 August

In the morning I walked down to the *gîte,* an attractive, traditional timber chalet perched above the river. The young guardian was sympathetic when I explained about my need to rest up for a few days and he gave me a pleasant room after the guests of the previous night had left. There was a sunlit garden at the front of the building and I sat there, reading or just day-dreaming. Inevitably my thoughts came back to my painful ankle and I now had grave doubts about my capacity to finish the journey. Looking at the maps, I could see that, although the mountain ranges were getting lower, the continuous up and down crossing of passes, ridges and crests went on all the way to the sea without let-up. It was going to stay hard.

I spent the day in low spirits, sitting in the garden or aimlessly wandering near the chalet and getting more and more frustrated at my immobility. In the evening a large party of French climbers appeared. The *gîte* was now full of friendly chat and banter and my spirits rose during an excellent shared supper, prepared by the guardian, a competent chef.

30 August

The others left early and the guardian sat down with me and told me a little about the area. La Chalp was the gateway to the Queyras region, an area best known for its wealth of wild flowers. These were in their greatest profusion in June and July, but there were still many late-flowering plants in the valleys and on the dolomitic mountain slopes. The region was also famous for its isolation and hard winters. Italy to the east and the rest of France to the west can be reached only by high passes, mostly blocked by snow for months. The inhabitants are independent spirits. Wood carving, born obviously from long winters indoors, is a local tradition. The Parc Naturel Regional du Queyras is one of the newer national parks in France and I hoped it would escape the ski menace.

Thoroughly fed up by late morning, I went down to the lower village of Arvieux. The traditional architecture of this little place was still well preserved: the combination of hay lofts, animal and human accommodation, knitted together by balconies and staircases, all built in timber on heavy stone bases, made satisfying drawings. I sat by the river and tried bathing my ankle in the icy water. This seemed to dull the pain and the swelling subsided.

I was alone in the *gîte* that night and resolved to go on the next day.

31 August

At this point I had walked over 2,000km, which should have been cause for celebration. Instead, I was deeply depressed. My ankle was worse than ever and I wondered if I could go on much farther. The next leg, to Ceillac, was more than 30km and involved 1,200m of climbing. I started early and made good progress until a point where the trail markers disappeared. By the time I had found the route again, I had added about a half-hour to what was going to be a very long day.

A steep eroded trail led down into the extraordinary little town of Château-Queyras, dominated by Vauban's massive fortifications. I marvelled at the prolific work of this great military engineer-architect, and the builders of these stupendous stone structures in such inaccessible mountain country. There was a story that Hannibal had camped at this spot on his way from Spain into Italy. I tried to imagine a line of elephants filing along these narrow tracks.

In what became known as the Second Punic War in 218 BC, the Carthaginian general began his campaign with 40,000 men and 38 elephants. Fighting his way across the Pyrenees he and his men then had to endure attacks from the Gauls in the Alps, where huge boulders were rolled down on them from the heights. Fresh snow and ice on the passes added to the difficulties of the epic expedition. Hannibal finally descended into Italy with 20,000 soldiers and 6,000 cavalry. Only a few of the elephants survived.

The early part of the long climb to the Col Fromage was up a dramatically rocky, narrow gorge which soon opened out into wide pastures with scattered pines and larches. The day had started warm and humid and there were all of the signs of a coming storm. A welcoming crest of a ridge appeared up high and when I came onto the top, I found that this was one of those maddening false summits that so often dash tired climbers' hopes. The real summit of the pass was at least a kilometre away and I could see black clouds boiling up to the west. The path traversed the slope above a deep valley and by the time I reached the col, the storm broke. Lightning crackled around me and the thunder banging overhead was deafening. It was a frightening experience crossing the pass, because the most dangerous place to be when lightning strikes is high ground.

I hurried away over the far side of the col, down to wide open, easy slopes which are far safer in storms. The deep valley, carved by the torrent of the Cristillian, was a long way below, half-hidden by the driving rain and torn clouds. In 1957 huge avalanches had devastated the valley and threatened the low villages and on the multiple zigzags of the track there were signs warning walkers not to take short cuts. When the gradient increased lower down, there was ample evidence of this erosion affecting the stability of the steep slope. I plodded down every switchback turn, wet and cold, and when the strain of worrying about being struck by lightning lifted, I was aware again of the pain in my ankle.

The town of Ceillac was awash when I hobbled into the centre and found the large, well-equipped *gîte*. It was crowded: climbers had all been driven off the mountains by the storm. I was drenched to the skin and had to strip off in a cold, concrete-floored ante-room and put all my wet clothes on a drying rack. Plastic bags had kept my spare clothes reasonably dry, however, and I was glad to move into a warm day room and sit near a red-hot stove.

My ankle was swollen and painful and I sat alone in a mood of near despair. It was only nine or ten days walk to Nice but I did not think my ankle would hold out. I went to bed not knowing what I was going to do.

1 September
This was my hundredth day on the journey. I awoke at 5.30 to ear-splitting thunder and looked out to see sheets of water

sweeping across the car park. The valley was filled with black clouds, and lightning lit up the early dawn. I tried to get out of my bunk and found my ankle had swollen like a balloon. The decision had been made for me. I would have to give up.

Taking a bus down the valley to Mont Dauphin seemed to be the only option. There was a railway station there and maybe I could get information about transport to Nice. A friendly group of three young French people had shared the room with me and they saw me fiddling with the elastic bandage on my ankle. They were abandoning their holiday and offered to give me a lift down to the lowlands. We set off in the heavy rain. Halfway down, on a bend under a precipice, the car hit a large rock on the road, presumably dislodged by the water pouring off the cliffs. The steering and transmission were badly damaged and we just managed to freewheel into a nearby village. After a couple of hours sheltering in a café with my new friends, who had to wait for a replacement car, I caught a bus down to Mont Dauphin.

The tourist centre was closed and I got conflicting information from a surly clerk at the station: there was no train anyway until the next day. A large café-bar nearby was crowded with people watching football on television and I could find nobody who could tell me how to get out of the place. The rain had stopped and I wandered about aimlessly, in confusion about what I should do and depressed at giving up the adventure after achieving so much. I realised that the long-distance trail was like a security blanket to me. Take it away and I was lost.

Sitting down on a low wall, I peeled off my ankle bandage and found that the swelling was not as bad as before, or at least I persuaded myself that it was better. A taxi pulled into the station forecourt and on an impulse I went over and asked the driver how much he would charge to take me back up the mountain. He said that he would have to telephone his boss to find out how much to charge and if it would be in order for him to make the long journey. We settled on a price which, although high, was not much more than it would cost to stay for a few nights in that dreary town. To save money and time, we took a shorter route back up the mountain which, although it would miss a small section of the official trail, would take me back on the route to Larche.

My morale was restored by this decision to go back. On the way up innumerable mountain bends, the thunder gradually died away and flashes of sunshine lit up green slopes. The taxi driver told me that the IRA had just announced that they had 'stopped the war', as he put it. This was another reason to lift my spirits and I felt like singing when the driver dropped me back on the trail and drove off. The contrast between the multiple disasters of the early morning and the renewed optimism of the brightening afternoon could not have been greater.

2 September

I found a hotel in the little high-mountain village of Larche which is right on the frontier of Italy and was destroyed by the retreating German army in 1944. Now restored, there was a small municipal building housing yet another of the exhibitions I had encountered on my journey, in memory of the fiftieth anniversary of the invasion of mainland Europe in June 1944. I was intrigued by one panel which hinted at the contempt which the Nazi garrisons of the Alpes-Maritimes had for the fighting quality of the Americans in the later landing on the Mediterranean coast. They were to get a rude shock when they encountered the invasion force and the display commemorated the enemy's defeat in the mountains by the Americans, helped by the French partisans. The black-and-white photographs made it all seem like ancient history and it was hard to imagine this beautiful place being racked by warfare. The numerous gun emplacements, however, half-hidden on the upper slopes above the village, were clear evidence of that violent period.

After the black despair of the previous day, the morning dawned more hopefully. The sky was showing signs of clearing and my ankle did not feel too bad. The early part of the walk up a wide beautiful valley was easy. For many days I had met few people on the trail and that morning I had the feeling, alone on the long path to the Pas de la Cavelle, that I was the one left behind; everybody else had gone home. So I was surprised when I came abruptly onto the sharp crest of the pass to find several small groups sheltering from the cold wind behind old stone fortifications. A young couple, students from the north of England, were the first English speakers I had met on the open trail.

The guidebook warned of the dangers of loose scree on the descent from the col and I was glad of my stick for balance, although it still felt that the whole steep slope could slide away. Over to the west the sky was jet black, and distant thunder echoed from the cliffs. I walked fast, now with a sense of urgency that another storm was on the way, across a delightful meadow lined with glacial moraines. An unexpected steep climb led to the Col des Fourches, covered with old concrete fortifications. The thunder and lightning now broke over me and I ran over the crest of the ridge to the safety of the other side. Curiously there was little rain and I quickly descended to the primitive stone refuge at Bouziéyas.

Several small parties stayed there that night and I enjoyed the company after so many lonely days. The English couple I had met on the pass arrived and the young man told me that they were also walking the GR5 all the way. He was more than a little disappointed to discover that the long-distance walk started in Holland and not at Lac Léman, being under the impression that he and his girlfriend were doing the route from the start! They were cheerful young people who were surviving on very little money, sleeping out where they could and living on food bought locally. It reminded me of my young days.

I crossed into the Maritime Alps that day and also into the Mercantour National Park. At the Pas de la Cavelle I was only 60km from the ocean as the crow flies. I was no crow and the mountain profile diagram in the guidebook was a shark's teeth of ascents and descents, still to be traversed.

3 September

An ice-blue sky greeted us after the storm and the sun picked out in sharp relief every ravine, cliff and crest on the mountains ringing the deep valley. My mood had gone from the despair of a few days before to sheer delight. My ankle felt a lot better and I could not wait to get started. As well as the young English couple, a small French group was also heading my way. It was comforting to have others on the same trail, to pass and be passed, exchange greetings and maybe meet each evening in a refuge. It had not happened to me for weeks.

I started slowly, however, to save my ankle, but also to savour being in the high mountains on such a perfect day. On the first pass, the Col de la Colombière, I rested for an hour in the sun and was joined for a while by my young English friends and we swapped stories about the journey and college life, they as students and me as a retired lecturer. They hurried on, leaving me lazing in the sunshine. My ankle was holding up well but was still swollen, so I tried to save it on the rocky descents.

The wild flowers were splendidly brilliant in pastures along the way, particularly large mauve crocuses. It was strange to see such typically spring flowers in early autumn, but then the alpine zones have their own cycle of flowering vegetation, where you can go from spring to summer and then to autumn, depending on the altitude and the orientation of the slope. Hundreds of butterflies fluttered along the way: large yellow types along with tiny bright blue ones and I was sure I saw a couple of gorgeous Painted Ladies. As I descended the south-facing slopes to Sainte-Etienne-de-Tinée, there was an occasional exotic swallowtail. On the final steep zigzags to the town, I really felt that I was entering the warm south at last; the noise of crickets was deafening, lizards darted across the path and the air scented with wild herbs.

When I booked into a little hotel in the town, the proprietor, commenting on my Irish nationality, said 'Ah, Tony Cascarino'. The Irish soccer player was now a member of the Marseilles team. It made a change from a comment about bombs.

That night I felt satisfied that my ankle was no worse after a reasonably long day and there was the delicious thought that in just a few days time I would see the Mediterranean.

4 September

It was hot in the morning. A lower altitude was probably one reason, but it was obvious that I was now far south. I started late for a short day but one which turned out to be as hard as any of the past long stretches. The road out of the town – a more colourful place than the drab alpine villages – ran past bright red roofs and yellow painted walls with trailing gaudy bougainvillea. Leaving the road, a steep track led to the upper ski resort of Auron through a claustrophobically thick forest. I was lathered in sweat before open meadows appeared over the crest of a ridge. It felt like a return to the humid tortures of the Vosges in early July.

Below the ridge, in a fine natural bowl, crouched the new resort of Auron. It was the usual mishmash of apartments, hotels, shopping arcades; the principal architectural monument being a large cable car station. I had given most of my available francs to the taxi driver for the long trip back up to the trail, so I had to search for a cash machine, the banks being closed for the Sabbath. Walking back up the street, I met my English friends from the previous days, John and Sue. They had been joined for the last part of the journey to Nice by Alison, an animated young design student, full of life and laughter.

Above the resort the landscape abruptly changed: gone were the signs of southern provinces and I was back into high alpine country. Dark conifers replaced the oaks and chestnuts and, worst of all, the ski-industry was busy ripping the heart out of the forested slopes. The marked trail vanished, wiped out by unnatural pistes, bulldozed straight down and oblivious to the weaving, gentle coutours of the old slopes. I struggled up the hellish mud scars and, finding no visible signs of the GR, struck out through an untouched area of forest, hoping to strike the right line for the Col du Blainon.

Struggling out through low branches, I saw the open slopes below the pass and in a steamy sweat sat down to rest on the crest. For the first time in weeks I was bothered by flies. Thousands of little black monsters covered my legs and arms and after a few minutes I fled from the summit in disgust. A cool breeze on the far side of the col blew them away and the rest of the path down to the *gîte* at Roya was a walker's dream, looping down across pastures of waving grasses, past ruined granges and cascading rivulets, until the roar of the torrent of the Roye signalled the end of the trail.

The fine timber *gîte* above the river was a welcome sight. I was enjoying the fellowship of the mountain refuges: anonymous hotels and lonely trails had me starved both for companions and conversation. Two of the French from the previous *gîte* at Bouziéyas were there, and later three young Parisians joined us.

5 September

I was the first away, after an early breakfast. The others, being not long on the trail, took ages to get themselves organised. Clothes were strewn over all of the spare bunks in the dormitory; rucksacks were packed and unpacked, 'Where is my fucking sock – boot – hat – sunglasses', arguments broke out over who last had what, while I smoothly and smugly strode off into the fresh morning.

A new mountain landscape opened up before me. The forests vanished and the rocky gorge of the Mairis led up to the valley of Sellevieille. This was a great bare landscape of denuded slopes and, higher up, I saw rivers of sheep flowing into stone enclosures. It was rounding-up time for the coming winter and I could hear the distant shouts of shepherds carried on the wind. A splendid path wound between gigantic boulders, remnants of glacial melting, then debouching abruptly onto a wide flat terrace: a superb hidden valley, green grassed and hemmed in by white limestone cliffs.

Finally, after a near 1,000m climb from Roya, I reached the

sharp crest of the Col de Crousette. I sat down in the shelter of a ruined sheepfold and gazed out to the new horizon. Before me, to the south, were layer after layer of pale silhouettes of ridges, all still to be crossed before journey's end. The difference, however, to the views from all the innumerable passes previously crossed, was that this was the last high col and from now on the crests in front would get lower and lower. I could not yet exult at this key moment as my last highest point was 100m higher up from the col, via a diagonally slanting path over the flanks of Mont Mounier.

The guidebook tempted me with the information that, from the summit of Mont Mounier, the Mediterranean could be seen. This would involve a detour of two hours on an already long day, so I resisted the temptation. There was also the thought that by postponing the delicious moment, the pleasure would be all the greater.

Below lay a landscape like those pictures from the moon. A great barren, inclined plane, littered with the detritus of long-vanished glaciers, offered a last, easy walk along a clearly marked trail to the saddleback of the Col de Moulinès. Accustomed to daily solitude, I was stretched out, half-asleep in the sun, when I was startled by a walker who appeared from the far side of the sharp crest, almost stepping on me. A fit-looking woman, with a heavy rucksack, greeted me and sat down nearby for a rest. We began a tentative conversation in French and it was a while before we both realised that it was not our own language. Jane Hoy was a Londoner and was walking the GR5 in the opposite direction for a few weeks. I think that we both felt the need for conversation and spent an agreeable hour discussing work, the perfidy of institutions, retirement and the sheer joy of liberty from a nine to five existence. It felt like a meeting of kindred spirits and we reluctantly said goodbye, as we went off in opposite directions.

The dramatic Portes de Longon was a true rocky gateway to the placid slopes of a high green valley, at the end of which was the Vacherie de Roure. This former, ancient stone farm and cowsheds had recently been renovated to include a little restaurant and *gîte* accommodation for walkers. I watched a splendid sunset as the three young Parisians of the previous evening arrived and joined me on the terrace.

6 September

Down, down, down. This was a day of descents, to the lowest point for some time, although the mountains were by no means finished. The high pastures ended at the lip of a steep gorge and the path was a dramatic series of zigzags, above a torrent and past spectacular cascades. The forests returned, but these were mature stands of occasionally majestic conifers, opening out to large clearings with meadows of long grasses and wildflowers. The deserted village of Rougois was a strange place: collapsing wood chalets and broken walls were signs of the declining old way of life of the alpine people.

The coniferous forest gave way to stands of oak and chestnut and lower down I passed through an area of old terraces with olive trees. I heard a bell and along the terrace below me an old man, flat black beret clamped firmly on his head, stalked past with a small herd of goats. The stone walls of the terraces were crumbling, the trees looked neglected and choked by undergrowth. I wondered if I was witnessing one of the last gasps of the old way of life in the rural south.

Just before the village of Roure there was a tiny chapel on the roadside, dedicated to Saint Sebastian. This early sixteenth-century building had contemporary frescoes depicting the martyrdom of the saint; images of near-naked bodies, shot with arrows and lots of blood, covered all the interior walls and vaulting. It was a doleful image on a bright mountainside where yellow butterflies fluttered and the white walls of the village sparkled nearby.

The valley of the Tinée, the river that parallelled and intersected the GR5 in the high mountains for so long, appeared again below, with the town of Sainte-Sauveur-sur-Tinée straggling along one bank. The municipal *gîte* was a primitive affair. There was no common room, only a gloomy kitchen. I escaped from the clatter of other residents, cooking their food, to a restaurant in the town and went to bed early.

Now that the journey was nearly over, I had mixed feelings. On the one hand, there was relief that the daily grind of hard physical effort and much discomfort would end, but there was also some sadness that I was leaving the beautiful mountains and that the sublime pleasures of early morning solitary walks, in exhilarating landscapes, where the dew was still on the ground, would soon be only a memory.

7 September

I could not find anyone to pay for my night's lodging so had to leave without paying. The whole town seemed to be asleep. From the low point of the valley the route followed an old rough road which traced a line across a wide cirque up to the hamlet of Rimplas. This extraordinary place, crowned by an old fortification, was perched on the tip of a belvedere, with sensational views.

It was getting hot when I left the village and the track was dusty, alive with lizards and butterflies and carpeted in places in fallen sweet chestnut leaves. The signs of autumn were everywhere, the grasses turning yellow and gold, with deep red foliage on the tangled scrub. The Provençal sun, however, was still scorching, even though the summer was nearly over – as was my long walk. On the way, when I crossed a surfaced road, I saw a signpost for Nice – 66km. The walking route was just about the same distance, but attacked the heights instead of flowing along the river valleys.

I passed the young Parisians, who were now slowly trailing along, affected by the heat and not yet fully fit. The last hour up to Saint-Dalmas-Valdeblore was a hot, sweaty tramp and I was glad to sit in the shade, on a terrace looking back down the pass. The municipal *gîte* was tucked away in the old centre and was deserted. I had to search for someone who was in charge and eventually found the appointed guardian, a genial man who opened up for me. I was joined later by two good-humoured Frenchmen, retired and enjoying their life of new freedom. They, and the Parisians who had also appeared, were not travelling along the GR5 to Nice but were walking an alternative, the GR52, which takes a longer, circuitous route towards the Italian frontier before ending on the coast at Menton.

The final challenge was just ahead. A long day's haul of eight to nine hours, traversing high rocky wilderness to the village of Utelle. I regretted not having company because I was more than slightly apprehensive of the way ahead. The weather forecast was not good and this area, I had heard, was notorious for the ferocity of its storms at this time of year. On top of that, there were no easy escape routes from the high crossing. Before bedtime I went out to look at the heights above. Dark clouds were settling on the tops and it did not look too healthy. I decided to start very early and try to beat any storm.

8 September
It was pitch dark when I got up at 5 a.m. and, frustratingly, since I was impatient to get started, there was only barely enough light at 6 a.m. to find my way on to the route. I had difficulty locating trail markings until a pale dawn allowed me to see ahead. The first part of the way was up a cruelly steep, rocky path which only relented at the Col de Varaire, the first of eight high passes I would have to cross before the safety of the village of Utelle.

The sky looked ominous, heavy steel-grey clouds turned almost jet black towards the west and, although it was warm when I had started, it began to feel unnaturally cold. I went fast, filled with urgency to get as far along the way before the weather broke. After the Col there was a long easy trail at high level, sometimes across steep flanks and more often along the limestone crests. The sky grew more and more threatening and I was getting really worried. I had walked for nearly four hours when I reached a halfway point at an old military barracks under the Col du Fort. Some of the ruined buildings had been rebuilt as a summer camp, but it was now deserted. The only possible escape route was down a long logging road to a valley which was way off my route. I paused to consider the best option. The cautious course would be to abandon the high level route and try to escape the storm by going down to the valley. This would spoil my plans for the final three days, so I decided to take a chance and press on. The weather was still holding.

The rain began after a sharp descent through a forest made me reluctant to retrace my steps. It gradually got worse and the lightning, which up to then had flickered in the distance, crackled around me and the thunder was almost continuous. I was soon soaked to the skin through my useless rainproof.

Coming on to the high rocky crests, which formed the last part of the trail, I was battered by the torrential rain and was really frightened by the lightning. High sharp ridges are about the most dangerous places to be in an electrical storm and this was the worst I had experienced in over 40 years mountaineering. Remembering all those stories about ice axes attracting lightning and buzzing like bees, I debated getting rid of my trek stick, but then what would I do on the steep descents? At one point a flash seemed to explode all around me and I was nearly blinded. The thunder was ear-splitting and I began to talk out loud to myself of the possibility of being suddenly struck dead. I began to accept that this might happen and since there was nothing I could do about it, I put my head down and walked on through the raging maelstrom.

Eventually the clouds were torn apart and I got a glimpse of stone buildings below. It was the village of Utelle and after eight hours of extreme effort I walked into the central square which seemed deserted and awash with water flowing from every roof, gutter and drain. I heard my name called and in a corner, huddled together under an overhang, were the young English threesome, looking bedraggled and disconsolate. They told me that they could not find the *gîte*. I hammered on the door of a shuttered café which opened to reveal an interior filled with people eating and drinking and having a good time. We drank bowls of hot chocolate and our clothes left pools of water on the floor. We were jubilant that we had passed the last test.

The barman offered to phone the guardian of the *gîte* and after a pleasant hour an important-looking woman appeared and insisted on taking us in her car the short distance to the building. We had the place to ourselves and the first thing we did was to put our wet clothes to dry over an electric heater. We had picked up some wine at the café and drank it with blankets draped around us in the steamy heat.

9 September

The morning dawned with a clear blue sky, as if there never had been a storm. All the mountain ridges around were sharply etched and the buildings shone in the clear light. My young friends were running out of both money and time and decided to make a long dash to reach Nice in one go. I wished them luck: as it was a trip of over ten hours walking. My rendezvous with Nuala and Cathie was on 11 September, so I had three days to complete the journey. I decided on the luxury of dawdling the last few kilometres and enjoying every step of the way – that is, if the weather held.

I turned to look back at Utelle and hardly recognised the place from the previous day. The bright stone buildings stood out in relief on the high promontory, commanding a wide panorama of rocky mountains and deep green valleys. The track down to the crossroads in the valley was an old muleteers' road and it hairpinned its way down by slopes that had the true look of Provence. There were stunted pines, fig trees and olives and at one point on the trail I almost stepped on a snake. There was an overpowering scent of aromatic herbs and the sky was deepening into that special cobalt blue of the Mediterranean.

The track went down and down, to the lowest point for weeks at 198m. One more sharp climb brought me to the town of Levens. Suddenly, there were no high mountains in front of me for the first time since leaving Lac Léman, only two low hills separated me from the sea. Arriving at midday, I found a room in a small hotel and sat down to lunch in a dining room where it looked as if all of the patrons were well over 80. There was only one man, and the dozen or so elderly women present looked expensively dressed. An eerie silence prevailed throughout the meal and the depressing thought was that these people had come there to die.

Shaking off these morbid thoughts, I went out to explore the pink and white delightful place with its narrow streets and sunlit squares. I gave myself the pleasure of a leisurely time for drawing, in a peaceful corner beside the seventeenth-century church.

That evening, after dinner, I lay on my bed and savoured the thought that I would see the Mediterranean in just a few hours. My first sight after over 2,200km. There was a local brass band practising in a hall near my window and they played

Levens

one phrase over and over again. It had a vaguely familiar yet exotic sound and I found it curiously haunting. Somehow it seemed to form a farewell anthem to my journey.

10 September
Shortly after leaving Levens, I was walking through a wood where the bushes were singing with crickets and lavender lined the path when, in a gap between the twisted pines, I saw a sliver of smoky blue. The Mediterranean at last! This was only a glimpse and I was impatient for the grand view. Along a track up to one of the last rises I met a party of jolly older walkers descending and their leader called out '*Ah, un randoneur.*' They stopped to chat to me and I suppose my weather-beaten appearance was a contrast to their impeccable sports clothes. They asked if I was walking the GR5 and were suitably amazed to hear I had come from the North Sea. They all insisted on shaking my hand.

A hot climb to near the summit of Mont Cima and there it was, the Mediterranean, a vista of intense blue all the way from Nice to Cap d'Antibes. I had made it at last. It seemed so long since I had left the cold grey waters beyond the dunes at the Hook of Holland. It had been four months to the day.

Aspremont, where I had planned to spend my last night, was an enchanting place: another old hill town, perched high on a rocky promontory, a colourful mix of warm stone, painted plaster and a jumble of red-tiled roofs. The town, with its concentric narrow streets, some only three metres wide, was built on this secure place as a protection from the Saracens, over 1,000 years before. The hotel owner, perhaps sensing the occasion, gave me a room with a balcony at the top of the building and a stunning view over the bay.

That night the hills beside Nice were a solid black, outlined sharply against a pink sunset. A harvest moon was reflected in the water and Venus was a bright dot in the western sky.

11 September
The final day. I left Aspremont on a splendid morning with the Maritime Alps behind me to the north, all purple and sharply

Aspremont, with the first view of the Mediterranean to the right drawn in the early sun. This, I reflected, was Cézanne country and I could sense the bold colours and forms of his beloved mountain of Provence, Sainte-Victoire, which he painted again and again, producing 30 oils and 45 watercolours of the peak. The intense blues of his pictures; cerulean, prussian and ultramarine could be sensed in the distant views while the wonderfully overlapping greens; viridian, olive and sap suffused the foreground. The approaching autumn tinted some of the flat planes of the Provence landscape from light sienna to dark umber.

The last walk was along the flanks of Mont Chauve d'Aspremont and it led across a landscape partly blackened by recent fires. Early on I heard gunshots ahead of me and realised that the hunting season had begun. This annual ritual slaughter of wildlife is a French obsession and I hoped I would not be one of the victims. A local paper had featured an article which claimed that 45 people had been shot dead the previous year and over 200 wounded by reckless hunters who fired at everything that moved. After the initial shots, I heard no more but saw small groups of hunters just standing around, possibly looking for something to shoot. I heard not a single bird. Had they killed them all?

When I had almost reached the top of the track, I met an impressive trio, each with a shotgun and bandoliers of cartridges draped across their camouflaged combat jackets. They looked as if they were about to invade somewhere. They were in great good humour, however, and stopped me with a cheerful greeting and enquired if I was 'wounded'. This referred to the bandage I was still wearing on my ankle. I assured them that I had not been shot, but it was the result of walking so far. They laughed at this and then told me they had killed nothing that morning because all the birds were gone. It did not seem to bother them as they sat there in the sunny morning, smoking and chatting.

For some time after I left Aspremont the sea was clearly visible and as the track wound gradually down the last slopes, past scorched rocks and still-smouldering charred bushes, my whole horizon was filled with the panorama of ocean. From up high it was the perfect journey's end.

When the path came into the town park above Nice, I saw a large party of hunters surrounding a thick patch of shrubbery and pointing their guns. I stopped in amazement to watch the scene as there were dozens of other people, including children, strolling the paths. It seemed unbelievable that shooting would be tolerated in this, albeit somewhat unkempt, town park. I was joined by another walker, also following the track from Aspremont, who remarked sourly to me that somebody had said that a bird was hiding there. He hoped that they would shoot themselves. I had to agree with him.

When the gate out of the park appeared, with the roadway leading down to the town centre, I sat on a rock in a grove of trees. I was early for our planned meeting and wanted to take time to reflect. The cold North Sea was far behind me and I remembered the highs of the journey; the first steep hills in the Ardennes; the Sunday morning walk above the sparkling waters of the Moselle; the springy turf of the high Vosges ridges and above all, that stunning first sight of Mont Blanc. The lows were now a distant memory; the doubts, despair and loneliness. My most powerful feeling was one of sadness that the long journey was over. For four months the walk had been my way of life and now my goal had been reached, but what next? In the final mountain stages the crossing of innumerable high passes was even more of a metaphor for attempting rediscovery of my lost youth than the journey south itself. The question I asked myself was 'Will I ever do anything like this again?' In the past, whenever I left a place where there was beauty and adventure, I wondered if I would ever return. This was my thought, looking out at the sublime sea.

The sense of excitement that the end of the journey provoked took over and I strode off down into the first suburbs. When the slope flattened out the canyons of streets blotted out the sea view. At the Place Alex Médicine Nuala and Cathie spotted me and came running to meet and warmly embrace.

The journey, however, was not properly finished until we had walked down past the tropical palms and yellow and pink

Promenade des Anglais, Nice

façades to the Promenade des Anglais. I picked my way over the stony beach and swam out into the warm blue Mediterranean.

A few days rest in Nice were a blur of sensations, swimming, eating, gallery visiting and sheltering from another storm and it was soon time to go. As the plane banked over the bay, I could see that all the summits and crests, stretching far to the north, were covered in fresh snow.

Winter had come to the mountains and I was going home.